D1580898

Was the Birth of Jesus According to Scripture?

Was the Birth of Jesus According to Scripture?

STEVE MOYISE

CASCADE *Books* · Eugene, Oregon

WAS THE BIRTH OF JESUS ACCORDING TO SCRIPTURE?

Cascade Books
An Imprint of Wipf and Stock Publishers
199 W. 8th Ave., Suite 3
Eugene, OR 97401

www.wipfandstock.com

ISBN 13: 978-1-62032-254-3

Cataloguing-in-Publication data:

Moyise, Steve.

   Was the birth of Jesus according to Scripture? / Steve Moyise.

   xviii + 98 pp. ; 23 cm. Includes bibliographical references.

   ISBN 13: 978-1-62032-254-3

   1. Jesus Christ—Nativity. 2. Bible. N.T.—Relation to the Old Testament. 3. Bible. O.T.—Quotations in the New Testament. 4. Virgin birth. 5. Bible. N.T. Gospels—Hermeneutics. 5. Bible—N.T.—Gospels—Criticism, interpretation, etc. I. Title.

BT2575.2 M69 2013

Manufactured in the U.S.A.

Permissions

Contents

Abbreviations

KJV	King James Version
LXX	Septuagint
NETS	New English Translation of the Septuagint
NIV	New International Version
NJB	New Jerusalem Bible
NRSV	New Revised Standard Version
RSV	Revised Standard Version

Introduction

EACH CHRISTMAS, CHURCHES THROUGHOUT the world celebrate the birth of Jesus through readings, carols, and nativity plays. A major feature of these events is that they are said to be fulfillments of Scripture. Thus according to Matthew's Gospel, Jesus' conception (1:23), place of birth (2:5-6), persecution by Herod (2:10), escape and return from Egypt (2:15), and settling in Nazareth (2:23) were all predicted by Israel's prophets (Isaiah, Micah, Jeremiah, Hosea). More generally, Matthew claims that Jesus was "the son of David, the son of Abraham" (1:1) by including a genealogy that traces his ancestry back to these two great Jewish figures. When Matthew introduces the quotation from Isa 7:14 with the words, "All this took place to fulfill what had been spoken by the Lord through the prophet" (1:22), he is effectively summarizing the rest of his gospel.[1]

Luke's Gospel begins with the claim that what he is about to narrate concerns "the events that have been fulfilled among us" (1:1). Included in these events are the angelic announcements of the births of John the Baptist (1:5-25) and Jesus (1:26-38), usually known as the annunciations. There is the *Magnificat* or song of Mary (1:46-55) and the *Benedictus* or song of Zechariah (1:68-79). And there is the witness of two elderly prophets, Simeon (2:29-35) and Anna (2:36-38). These stories are then followed by a genealogy that not only traces Jesus' ancestry back to David and Abraham but all the way back to Adam (3:23-38). Although Luke's Gospel has less formal quotations than Matthew,[2] it ends with Jesus telling his disciples

---

1. There are approximately sixty quotations in Matthew, drawn mainly from Isaiah (eleven), the Minor Prophets (ten), Deuteronomy (ten), and Psalms (nine). For a brief overview of Matthew's use of Scripture, see Moyise, *Old Testament in the New*, 34-44.

2. Luke includes around twenty-five quotations, mainly drawn from Psalms (seven), Isaiah (five), and Deuteronomy (five). See Moyise, *Old Testament in the New*, 45-62.

"everything written about me in the law of Moses, the prophets, and the psalms must be fulfilled" (24:44).

However, these claims raise a number of questions today. Firstly, if we look up the texts quoted by Matthew, some of them do not appear to be prophecies at all. Hosea 11:1 ("out of Egypt I called my son") and Jer 31:15 ("A voice is heard in Ramah, lamentation and bitter weeping") are references to Israel's exodus and exile respectively, and do not contain any future promises. The text that is said to support Jesus' settling in Nazareth in Matt 2:23 ("He will be called a Nazorean") cannot be found in any biblical manuscript known to us, and the wording of many of the quotations differs significantly from the original texts. For example, the NRSV renders the first part of Isa 7:14 as, "Look, the young woman is with child and shall bear a son," but Matt 1:23 reads, "Look, *the virgin shall conceive* and bear a son." If Matthew's quotations differ from the original texts, can we really speak about fulfillment?[3]

Second, Matthew and Luke are often our only sources for the events that they narrate. If we ask whether Herod really did murder "all the children in and around Bethlehem who were two years old or under" (Matt 2:16), then it has to be acknowledged that there is no reference to it in any other document of the period, including the rest of the New Testament. Some would argue that *if* such a catastrophic event really happened, it would surely have been recorded by someone. Indeed, we rely on historians such as Josephus for many of the details of Herod's reign, but he makes no mention of this. Perhaps Matthew invented the story in order to support the claim that the birth of Jesus was according to Scripture? On the other hand, it has been estimated that the population of Bethlehem was only about a thousand at the time and so the number of children under two might have been no more than twenty or thirty. Their deaths would of course be tragic but not necessarily newsworthy, given the level of atrocities in those days. Thus care must be taken when using such "arguments from silence," but it remains true that Matthew and Luke are often our only sources for the events being narrated, and their historical accuracy cannot be assumed.[4]

Third, there are differences between Matthew and Luke, both in detail and in overall approach. In terms of detail, one only has to compare the two

3. In the case of Isa 7:14, the differences are partly explained by the fact that Matthew is following a Greek text that used the specific word for "virgin" (*parthenos*), whereas the Hebrew uses a more general word for "young woman" (*almah*).

4. Bishop Spong claimed in 1992 that "no recognized New Testament scholar, Catholic or Protestant, would today seriously defend the historicity of these narratives" (*Born of a Woman*, 44) but this is certainly not true today, as we shall see.

genealogies to see a number of differences. For example, Matthew divides his genealogy into three groups of fourteen (1:17) and says that Joseph's father—Jesus' grandfather—was called Jacob (1:16). Luke has many more names in his genealogy and says that Joseph's father was called Heli (3:23). Various attempts have been made to explain this, as we shall see in due course, but it shows that our study cannot simply be a weaving together of the material in Matthew and Luke. The two gospels offer very different accounts of Jesus' birth and this is true of their overall approaches. The only texts that Luke actually quotes are to confirm that Mary and Joseph followed the precepts of the law by offering "a pair of turtledoves or two young pigeons" (2:24) for the birth of their child (Lev 12:8). Luke's approach to fulfillment is either by allusion, as when Mary says, "My soul magnifies the Lord, and my spirit rejoices in God my Savior" (1:46–47)[5] or by telling the stories in such a way that they evoke well-known stories from Scripture. For example, the story of God granting a child to the righteous but barren woman Elizabeth (1:7) clearly echoes the stories of Sarah (Gen 17:17) and Hannah (1 Sam 1:2).

Indeed, there is material like this in Matthew also. The story of Herod murdering the young children of Bethlehem (often known as the "slaughter of the innocents") is clearly intended as a parallel to the story of Pharaoh murdering the Hebrew children in Exod 1:22 ("Every boy that is born to the Hebrews you shall throw into the Nile"). The parallel continues with Jesus' sojourn in Egypt and then his departure, which Matthew explicitly claims to be a fulfillment of Hos 11:1 ("out of Egypt I called my son"). Such parallels are generally known as "typology," from the Greek word *typos*, meaning "pattern" or "example." An explicit example occurs in John 3:14–15, where Jesus says: "And just as Moses lifted up the serpent in the wilderness, *so must* the Son of Man be lifted up, that whoever believes in him may have eternal life." The major debate is whether such parallels or correspondences can in any sense be classed as fulfillment. There is nothing in the stories of Pharaoh seeking to kill the Hebrew children or the barren Hannah becoming pregnant that "predict" future events. But is prediction a necessary requirement for the concept of fulfillment?

Some would say Yes, arguing that Matthew and Luke have simply chosen to narrate the stories of Jesus in ways that imitate key figures and events in Scripture. This is clearly important for the way that readers understand

5. Ps 34:3 ("O magnify the LORD with me, and let us exalt his name together"); Ps 35:9 ("Then my soul shall rejoice in the LORD, exulting in his deliverance").

the stories but has no bearing on whether Jesus' birth was a fulfillment of Scripture or not. Others, however, are prepared to accept that a later event might be said to "fulfill" an earlier one if there is a sense of "fullness" or "completion" to it. For example, if it is true that Jesus came to deliver people from their sins, as Matt 1:21 claims, this could be seen as the fulfillment of the original exodus, where people were delivered from their physical bondage. Of course, this is a circular argument. For those who do not believe that Jesus can deliver people from their sins, the parallel is artificial and hence irrelevant to the question. But for those who accept this belief, it is a possible line of reasoning. Crossan and Borg, for example, are prepared to speak of the birth stories as fulfillment because Jesus "decisively reveals and incarnates the passion of God as disclosed in the Law and the Prophets—the promise and hope for a very different kind of world from the world of Pharaoh and Caesar, the world of domination and empire."[6] They do not, however, regard any of Matthew's five quotations as predicting the actual events of Jesus' birth.

How then shall we proceed? We could work our way through Matthew's infancy narratives and evaluate any claims (explicit or implicit) that are made, and then do the same for Luke. However, this sort of material can be found in the larger commentaries and is also the approach of Raymond Brown's famous work, *The Birth of the Messiah*.[7] Now in a second updated edition, Brown devotes over 700 pages to discussing the infancy narratives of Matthew and Luke and is the point of departure for studies written since that time. It is also the approach of the *Commentary on the New Testament Use of the Old Testament*, edited by Greg Beale and Don Carson,[8] and we will be drawing on the chapter on Matthew (Craig Blomberg). Our approach, however, will be different. Rather than commenting on each of the quotations and allusions as they arise, we will take a more thematic approach, looking at the claims that Jesus was preceded by a forerunner (chapter 1) and was not only a descendant of David (like Joseph and many others) but was the promised "son of David" (chapter 2). We will then look at the question of whether Jesus' birth in Bethlehem, flight and return from Egypt, and settling in Nazareth are credible as historical events and whether they can be

6. Crossan and Borg, *The First Christmas*, 224.

7. Brown, *The Birth of the Messiah*. All references are to the updated edition, 1993.

8. This is an extremely useful source book, examining the quotations and major allusion under the following headings: (A) NT; (B) OT context; (C) Use in Jewish Sources; (D) Textual background; (E) Hermeneutic employed; and (F) Theological use.

understood as fulfillments of Scripture (chapters 3–4). Also in these chapters we will consider the visit of the magi and their three gifts (tradition speaks of the three wise men but the text does not say that they were wise or that there were three of them), the guiding star, and the slaughter of the innocents. In chapter 5, we tackle the question that has dominated discussion down the centuries: the claim that Jesus was born of a virgin and that this fulfills the prophecy of Isa 7:14.

It will soon become clear that however objective we try to be, questions like whether Jesus was the promised "son of David" or "born of a virgin" are inevitably influenced by one's overall assessment of his significance. If one thinks of him as a well-meaning but ultimately misguided teacher or prophet, it is unlikely that one will conclude that he is the ruler promised in Mic 5:2, whatever Matthew says. And if one thinks that scientific laws are immutable, clearly one will not accept the notion of a guiding star or a conception without a human father. However, it is important to note that the alternative does not necessarily involve taking everything in Matthew and Luke literally. For example, it was already obvious to John Chrysostom, Archbishop of Constantinople in the fourth century, that a star is far too high in the sky to point to a particular house in Bethlehem. Most commentators today believe that Matthew is talking about a supernatural guidance that was real to the magi (if they existed) but did not consist of planets leaving their orbits or stars changing their trajectories. It is possible that other events, such as the slaughter of the innocents or the virginal conception of Jesus might be similarly understood, as Crossan and Borg argue.

Before we begin, it is worth situating the infancy narratives between two other sets of writings, one just before the Gospels of Matthew and Luke were written (thought to be around 75–85 C.E.) and one a half a century or so later. The first consists of the letters of Paul, written between about 49–64 C.E., and the Gospel of Mark, written shortly before or after the destruction of Jerusalem by the Romans in 70 C.E.[9] These writings show no interest in the circumstances of Jesus' birth and the few comments made about his family or lineage appear to assume that it was quite normal. For example, Paul says in Gal 4:4–5:

---

9. Most writers now use the abbreviations C.E. (Common Era) and B.C.E. (Before the Common Era) rather than the traditional B.C. and A.D. in recognition that Jesus' birth initiated a period where Jews and Christians co-exist together, as Paul made clear in Rom 9–11.

> But when the fullness of time had come, God sent his Son, *born of a woman, born under the law,* in order to redeem those who were under the law, so that we might receive adoption as children. (Gal 4:4–5).

Later Christian doctrine will understand the phrase, "God sent his Son," as a reference to the incarnation but Paul's point is that Christ had to be born under the law in order to redeem those under the law. Although he says nothing about the actual conception of Jesus, it is hard to imagine him pursuing such an argument if he thought that it was fundamentally different from everyone else. Indeed, earlier in his letter, he can speak of James as "the Lord's brother" (1:19) without any need for qualification.

The same can be said for Mark's references to Jesus' family. In the incident of Mark 3:31–35, the crowd say to Jesus: "Your mother and your brothers and sisters are outside, asking for you" (3:32). Jesus then makes the point that his "family" is not governed by physical connection but embraces all who do the will of God (3:35). The contrast would make little sense if there was not in fact a physical connection between Jesus and the brothers and sisters who are waiting outside. The point is even clearer in the so-called "rejection in Nazareth" story:

> On the sabbath he began to teach in the synagogue, and many who heard him were astounded. They said, "Where did this man get all this? What is this wisdom that has been given to him? What deeds of power are being done by his hands! *Is not this the carpenter, the son of Mary and brother of James and Joses and Judas and Simon, and are not his sisters here with us?"* And they took offense at him. (Mark 6:2–3).

Although it may be significant that Joseph is not mentioned here,[10] the point of their objection is that they think that Jesus is "getting ideas above his station." As far as they are concerned, he is a simple villager like them; they grew up with him and they know his brothers and sisters. Jesus' reply is not that he is different from everyone else by virtue of a miraculous birth but the proverb, "Prophets are not without honor, except in their hometown, *and among their own kin,* and in their own house" (6:4).

However, there is one thing that is important about Jesus' birth and that is his descent from David. Mark shows this by having a blind beggar address Jesus as "son of David" (10:47) and an adoring crowd welcoming him

---

10. It could be that Joseph died soon after the birth of Jesus or that there were rumors that Jesus was illegitimate. We will discuss this in more detail in chapter 5.

6

to Jerusalem with the words: "Blessed is the coming kingdom of our ancestor David! Hosanna in the highest heaven!" (11:10). For Paul, it is his statement at the beginning of the letter to the Romans that is particularly significant:

> Paul, a servant of Jesus Christ, called to be an apostle, set apart for the gospel of God, which he promised beforehand through his prophets in the holy scriptures, the gospel concerning his Son, *who was descended from David according to the flesh* and was declared to be Son of God with power according to the spirit of holiness by resurrection from the dead, Jesus Christ our Lord . . . (Rom 1:1–4)

There has been much debate as to whether Paul is saying that the resurrection *confirmed* the identity of Jesus as "Son of God" or that it *established* it, but for our purposes, it is the first clause that is important: Jesus was descended from David "according to the flesh." The emphasis on "according to the flesh" makes it difficult to believe that Paul thought Jesus was conceived without a human father.[11] Instead, his point is that he thinks that Jesus meets both the physical and spiritual requirements to be God's Messiah.

All this is in contrast with the literature that came after Matthew and Luke. In the *Infancy Gospel of James*, we are given the following additional information: Mary's birth was also miraculous; she was pure and grew up in the temple; and she continued to show the signs of virginity even after Jesus' birth:[12]

> And so Joachim came with his flocks, while Anna stood at the gate. Then she spotted Joachim approaching with his flocks and rushed out and threw her arms around his neck: "Now I know that the Lord God has blessed me greatly. This widow is no longer a widow, and I, once childless, am now pregnant." (4:8–9)

> When the child turned three years of age, Joachim said, "Let's send for the undefiled Hebrew daughters. Let them each take a lamp and light it, so the child won't turn back and have her heart captivated by things outside the temple." . . . The priest welcomed her, kissed her, and blessed her: "The Lord God has exalted your name among all generations. In you the Lord will disclose his redemption to the people of Israel during the last days." And he sat her down on the third step of the altar, and the Lord showered favor on her. And she danced, and the whole house of Israel loved her. (7:4–5, 7–10)

11. One could perhaps argue that "according to the flesh" would still be true if Jesus only had one parent but it is surely contrary to the thrust of the passage.

12. The following texts are taken from Miller (ed.), *The Complete Gospels*, 369–96.

> The midwife entered and said, "Mary, position yourself for an examination." . . . and Salome inserted her finger into Mary. And then Salome cried aloud and said, "I'll be damned because of my transgression and my disbelief; I have put the living God on trial. Look! My hand is disappearing! It's being consumed by flames!" . . . Salome approached the child and picked him up with these words: "I'll worship him because he's been born to be king of Israel." And Salome was instantly healed and left the cave vindicated. (20:1–4, 10–11)

In the *Infancy Gospel of Thomas*, not to be confused with the collection of Jesus' sayings known as the *Gospel of Thomas*, we find a number of stories from Jesus' childhood:

> When this boy, Jesus, was five years old, he was playing at the ford of a rushing stream. He was collecting the flowing water into ponds and made the water instantly pure. He did this with a single command. He then made soft clay and shaped it into twelve sparrows. . . . "Be off, fly away, and remember me, you who are now alive!" And the sparrows took off and flew away noisily. (2:1–3, 6)

> When he was six years old, his mother sent him to draw water and bring it back to the house. But he lost his grip on the pitcher in the jostling of the crowd, and it fell and broke. So Jesus spread out the cloak he was wearing and filled it with water and carried it back to his mother. (11:1–3)

> Now Jesus' father was a carpenter, making ploughs and yokes at that time. He received an order from a rich man to make a bed for him. When one board of what is called the crossbeam turned out shorter than the other . . . Jesus stood at the other end and grabbed hold of the shorter board, and, by stretching it, made it the same length as the other. (13:1–2a, 3)

> Joseph sent his son James to tie up some wood and carry it back to the house, and the child Jesus followed. While James was gathering the firewood, a viper bit his hand. And as he lay sprawled out on the ground, dying, Jesus came and blew on the bite. Immediately the pain stopped, the animal burst apart, and James got better on the spot. (16:1–2)

What this tells us is that there was a growing interest in understanding the whole of Jesus' life, including his parents and early childhood, as miraculous. In other words, when studying the birth of Jesus, there is a trajectory from little or no interest (Paul, Mark), to some interest (Matthew, Luke), to great interest (Infancy Gospels of James and Thomas). If we extend this period to the sixth century C.E. and beyond, we find in a work known as *Pseudo-Matthew* the following:[13]

> And on the third day after the birth of our Lord Jesus Christ, Mary went out of the cave and, entering a stable, placed the child in the manger, and an ox and an ass adored him. Then was fulfilled that which was said by Isaiah the prophet, "The ox knows his owner, and the ass his master's crib." [Isa 1:3] Therefore, the animals the ox and the ass, with him in their midst, incessantly adored him. Then was fulfilled that which was said by Habakkuk the prophet, saying, "Between two animals you are made manifest." [Hab 3:2 LXX](14)

> And on the journey there were with Joseph three boys, and with Mary a girl. And behold, suddenly there came out of the cave many dragons; and when the boys saw them they cried out in great terror. Then Jesus got down from his mother's lap and stood on his feet before the dragons; and they worshipped Jesus and then departed. Then was fulfilled that which was said by David the prophet, "Praise the Lord from the earth, dragons, and all you ocean depths." [Ps 148:7] (18)

It is easy to dismiss such stories as apocryphal, but how should we regard the stories in Matthew and Luke? Are they of the same ilk or does their earlier date locate them towards the beginning of the trajectory, where there was still *some* interest in historical details? I shall not try to answer this in advance, but suffice to say that there are reputable scholars on both sides of the debate. I have purposely chosen to move from the less controversial claims (Jesus was preceded by a forerunner) to the more controversial claims (Jesus was born without a human father) to keep the discussion as open as possible, but it will soon become clear that decisions have to be made. It is not my aim to make these decisions for you but I hope what follows will help to clarify the issues. In such a controversial area, this is the best that I can hope for.

---

13. Text from Elliott, *The Apocryphal New Testament*, 94. He notes that much "medieval art is indecipherable without reference to books such as Pseudo-Matthew" (84).

1

Preceded by a Forerunner

INTRODUCTION

THE BIRTH OF JOHN the Baptist is not mentioned in Matthew's infancy narrative but it plays a significant role in Luke. The gospel begins by referring to the "events that have been fulfilled among us" (1:1) and his first story is the announcement to a priest called Zechariah that his wife Elizabeth "will bear you a son, and you will name him John" (1:13). We are told that they were a devout couple, "righteous before God" and "living blamelessly according to all the commandments" (1:6). However, they had no children for Elizabeth was barren. We are immediately reminded of stories in Scripture where barrenness is overcome by God and "children of promise" are born. In particular, the reference to the couple's old age (1:7) puts one in mind of Abraham and Sarah (Gen 11:30), while the angel's instruction that the child "must never drink wine or strong drink" (1:15) parallels the births of Samson (Judg 13:2) and Samuel (1 Sam 2:11). Clearly the child will be an important figure in Israel's history but his role is said to be preparatory:

> You will have joy and gladness, and many will rejoice at his birth, for he will be great in the sight of the Lord. He must never drink wine or strong drink; even before his birth he will be filled with the Holy Spirit. He will turn many of the people of Israel to the Lord their God. With the spirit and power of Elijah *he will go before him*, to turn the hearts of parents to their children, and the disobedient

11

> to the wisdom of the righteous, *to make ready a people prepared for the Lord.* (Luke 1:14–17)

Zechariah found this difficult to believe and was struck dumb until the moment of John's birth. He was then filled with the Holy Spirit and uttered a prophecy that God was fulfilling the promises to Abraham and the patriarchs, so that his people might "serve him without fear, in holiness and righteousness before him all our days" (1:74–75). Zechariah then says this about his son:

> And you, child, will be called the prophet of the Most High; for you will *go before the Lord to prepare his ways*, to give knowledge of salvation to his people by the forgiveness of their sins. By the tender mercy of our God, the dawn from on high will break upon us, to give light to those who sit in darkness and in the shadow of death, to guide our feet into the way of peace. (1:76–79)

The pattern of the announcement of a son, a description of his birth, the giving of a name, and a prophecy concerning his significance is also used to introduce Jesus. First, the angel appears to Mary and announces that she will conceive and bear a son (1:31). However, he will not simply be "prophet of the Most High" but "Son of the Most High, and the Lord God will give him the throne of his ancestor David" (1:32). Second, his birth is described and an angel says to some nearby shepherds, "to you is born this day in the city of David a Savior, who is the Messiah, the Lord" (2:11). Eight days after his birth, the child is named (2:21), and when he is later presented in the temple, Simeon utters these words:

> This child is destined for the falling and the rising of many in Israel, and to be a sign that will be opposed so that the inner thoughts of many will be revealed—and a sword will pierce your own soul too. (2:34–35)

Although Jesus will be superior to John ("Son of God" rather than "prophet of God") and John's role is said to be preparatory, it is not yet clear that John is to be the forerunner of Jesus. This emerges in the stories that follow, beginning with John's announcement that his vocation is to fulfill the words of Isa 40:3: "The voice of one crying out in the wilderness: 'Prepare the way of the Lord, make his paths straight'" (Luke 3:4). Some commentators think that "Lord" here refers to Jesus but it probably still retains its original meaning of "God." John is to prepare the way for God's saving action by pointing to one who is greater than himself, who will baptize not with water but with the Holy Spirit (3:16). That person is made known to him when Jesus comes for baptism; the Holy Spirit descends upon him like a dove and a voice from heaven declares: "You are my Son, the Beloved; with you I am well pleased" (3:22).

However, John is unable to witness what happens next, for Herod has had him arrested (3:19). Languishing in prison, he seeks reassurance by sending disciples to ask Jesus: "Are you the one who is to come, or are we to wait for another?" (7:19). Jesus replies by citing a number of texts from Isaiah: "Go and tell John what you have seen and heard: the blind receive their sight, the lame walk, the lepers are cleansed, the deaf hear, the dead are raised, the poor have good news brought to them" (7:22).[1] Jesus then says to the crowd: "This is the one about whom it is written, 'See, I am sending my messenger ahead of you, who will prepare your way before you'" (7:27). The words are from Mal 3:1 and are closely linked with the prophecy of a returning Elijah (Mal 4:5–6). They are echoed in the song of Zechariah recorded in Luke 1:17: "With the spirit and power of Elijah he will go before him . . . to make ready a people prepared for the Lord." Thus Luke claims that John is the forerunner of Jesus and such a role is a fulfillment of Scripture.

Matthew and Mark have an additional story where Jesus discusses the meaning of the phrase, "Elijah must come first" (Matt 17:10–13; Mark 9:11–13). The source of the phrase is Mal 4:5–6 and Jesus endorses the view that Elijah does indeed come first to "restore all things." However, he then asserts that Elijah has already come, "and they did to him whatever they pleased, as it is written about him" (Mark 9:13). Mark leaves the reader to deduce that Jesus is talking about John the Baptist, whose death has just been narrated (6:17–29) but Matthew makes it explicit: "Then the disciples understood that he was speaking to them about John the Baptist" (Matt 17:13; Luke omits this story). Thus the claim that John is the forerunner of Jesus and that such a role is according to Scripture is supported by Matthew, Mark, and Luke.

In order to examine this claim, we will need to consider three things. First, what does Scripture say about a forerunner who prepares the way for

---

1. The main texts are Isa 29:18 ("On that day the deaf shall hear the words of a scroll, and out of their gloom and darkness the eyes of the blind shall see"); 35:5–6 ("Then the eyes of the blind shall be opened, and the ears of the deaf unstopped; then the lame shall leap like a deer, and the tongue of the speechless sing for joy"); and 61:1 ("the LORD has anointed me; he has sent me to bring good news to the oppressed, to bind up the brokenhearted, to proclaim liberty to the captives, and release to the prisoners").

God's coming and how is this figure related to the hope of Elijah's return? Second, what is the evidence that John the Baptist fulfills either or both of these roles? This is partly a question of historical evidence and partly a question of biblical interpretation. What sort of use of Scripture are we dealing with and is it a plausible interpretation of the texts? Third, what is the status of Luke's stories about John's birth? Are we to take them literally or should they be understood as narrative parables and if so, how does this affect the question of whether John's birth was according to Scripture?[2] We turn first to the question of what Scripture says about a coming figure, who will have a preparatory role to the main eschatological event, and thus act as a forerunner.

WHAT DOES SCRIPTURE SAY ABOUT A FORERUNNER?

Although the rabbis have much to say about the return of Elijah, there is only one text in the Hebrew Bible that specifically refers to it. After speaking about a future "messenger of the covenant" who will prepare the way for God's coming (Mal 3:1), the book of Malachi ends with these words: "Lo, I will send you the prophet Elijah before the great and terrible day of the LORD comes. He will turn the hearts of parents to their children and the hearts of children to their parents, so that I will not come and strike the land with a curse" (4:5–6). The prophecy draws on 2 Kgs 2:11, which says that, "Elijah ascended in a whirlwind into heaven," although nothing is said about any return. It is of interest that the Septuagint (LXX) rendered Malachi's "turn the hearts" clause as "restore the heart" and "sons to their fathers" as "person to his neighbor."[3] The effect is to change the emphasis from family harmony to the restoration of the covenant: Elijah will call Israel back to the way of life commanded by God in order to avert the coming wrath.

The next we hear of such a claim is in the book of Sirach, also known as Ecclesiasticus. Scholars think this was written about 200–175 B.C.E. and is one of the additional books included in the LXX but omitted from the

2. "To state our interpretive decision, we best understand the nativity stories and their meanings by treating them as neither fact nor fable, but as *parable*." (Crossan and Borg, *First Christmas*, 32).

3. Quotations from the Septuagint are taken from Pietersma and Wright (eds.), *New English Translation of the Septuagint*.

Hebrew canon. In a section celebrating the deeds of Elijah, we read: "He who was taken up in a whirlwind of fire and in a chariot of fiery horses. He who was recorded ready for the times, to calm anger before wrath, to turn the heart of a father to a son and to restore the tribes of Iakob" (Sir 48:9–10). This is clearly dependent on the Malachi text but with a number of differences. First, the clause about averting God's curse on the land has been summarized/interpreted as calming God's anger. Second, it follows the LXX of Malachi in speaking of "restoring" rather than "turning," but the object is now specifically the "tribes of Iakob." This is probably drawn from Isa 49:6, where God's servant will "raise up the tribes of Jacob" and "restore the survivors of Israel." Thus Elijah's role in the book of Sirach is to restore the dispersed tribes of Israel in preparation for the coming of God.

Given its emphasis on eschatological figures, it is surprising that there is only one mention of Elijah in the Dead Sea Scrolls. It comes in a fragmentary text (4Q558) where only the words, "therefore I will send Elijah befo[re]," are present. When this text was first published, Jean Starcky conjectured that a reference to the Messiah followed these words but there is no evidence for this; it is just as likely that it simply repeats the words of Malachi.[4] There is one other text (5Q521) where Elijah is not named but the saying, "for it is sure; fathers are coming upon their sons," is probably an allusion to the Malachi text. If this is the case, then it is possible that the one who raises the dead and brings good news to the poor, mentioned earlier in the fragment, is thought to be Elijah. On the other hand, the reference to bringing "good news to the poor" is almost certainly an allusion to the "anointed" servant of Isa 61:1, which appears to be the main source of the description.[5]

The only other source for understanding what was believed about Elijah in the first century is the New Testament itself. Thus in Herod's desire to understand how Jesus is able to work miracles (Mark 6:15), three suggestions are put forward: (1) John the Baptist has risen from the dead; (2) Jesus is Elijah; (3) Jesus is a prophet. Herod thinks the first is more likely since he himself had John put to death. Whether such a discussion ever took place is impossible to determine but the ambiguity over the role of Elijah is probably correct. It appears again when Jesus asks his disciples what people

4. Starcky, "Les Quatres Étapes du Messianisme," 487–505.

5. Jassen (*Mediating the Divine*, 148) accepts the identification with Elijah, stating that the "general character of Elijah's eschatological responsibilities" is preserved. However, he then notes that (1) The functions attributed to the figure far exceed what is said in Malachi and (2) the figure is the central protagonist and neither precedes or announces any other figure.

are saying about him. They respond with the same set of choices: "And they answered him, 'John the Baptist; and others, Elijah; and still others, one of the prophets'" (Mark 8:28). It would appear that the hope of Elijah's return was well known but there was no agreement on what role he would play.

Elijah is also mentioned in the transfiguration story and seems to be the reason why the disciples are puzzled about the scribal saying that "Elijah must come first." If Elijah has just appeared on the mountain with Jesus and Jesus is the promised Messiah, then Elijah did not come first. The answer given by Mark is that Elijah is not Jesus, as some were concluding, but John the Baptist, who did of course come first. Whether this exchange represents Jesus' explanation or is a later rationalization by Mark (or those before him), it reinforces the view that the returning Elijah was thought to have some sort of preparatory role, although it precise nature was unclear.

A further reference occurs in the crucifixion story where Jesus' cry from the cross is understood by the bystanders as a call to Elijah. According to Mark, Jesus uttered the first words of Ps 22:1 in the form, "Eloi, Eloi, lema sabachthani?" (15:34). For the benefit of his Greek speaking readers, he offers a translation of the words ("My God, my God, why have you forsaken me?") but the bystanders appear to have taken the cry, "Eloi, Eloi," as a reference to "Elijah." Matthew's version is slightly clearer in that he quotes the saying in Hebrew, where "My God, my God" is "Eli, Eli."[6] However, the point for our investigation is that having given Jesus a drink, the crowd say: "Wait, let us see whether Elijah will come to take him down" (Mark 15:36). This sounds like the belief found in later rabbinic sources[7] that Elijah comes to the aid of the righteous, but could it be more than that? According to Rikki Watts, the crowd would have known that Ps 22 moves from despair to hope and would thus take Jesus' words as a cry for deliverance, prompting them to think of Elijah.[8] Most scholars, however, think that this detracts from the main point of Mark's crucifixion account, namely, that at the moment of Jesus' death, he identifies with the *despair* of the psalmist, not the *hope* that comes later in the psalm.[9]

In summary, it is clear that there was a strong belief in Elijah's return but very little clarity on his role. The possibility that Jesus might be Elijah

---

6. The Aramaic targum that has come down to us also has "Eli Eli" but "Eloi Eloi" would be a possible rendering in Aramaic.

7. b. 'Abodah Zarah 17b; b. Ta'anit 21a.

8. Watts, "Mark," 237.

9. So Blomberg, "Matthew," 100.

suggests that some thought the returning Elijah would perform miracles, as the original Elijah did. The conversation following the transfiguration suggests that others thought in terms of a preparatory role, though there is no early evidence that this is specifically to prepare for the Messiah. The misunderstanding of his words at the crucifixion suggests that the later rabbinic view that Elijah comes to the aid of the righteous was known in the first century, although there is dispute as to what prompted the words. This lack of clarity will make it difficult to decide whether John fulfills the role of the coming Elijah and is perhaps why Luke speaks more generally of John coming in the "spirit and power of Elijah" (1:17).

What of the hopes inspired by Isa 40:3 ("In the wilderness prepare the way of the LORD, make straight in the desert a highway for our God")? The literal meaning concerns an actual path through the desert so that the exiles can return to their homeland. In this respect, it echoes an earlier text where God says to the exodus generation: "I am going to send an angel in front of you, to guard you on the way and to bring you to the place that I have prepared" (Exod 23:20). Both texts are probably in mind when Malachi says to his generation: "See, I am sending my messenger to prepare the way before me, and the Lord whom you seek will suddenly come to his temple" (Mal 3:1). This is interesting in that the "way" is no longer a literal path but a "way of life." It is also of note that the preparation is now associated with judgment rather than salvation, as is clear from the following verse ("But who can endure the day of his coming, and who can stand when he appears?").

Isaiah 40:3 was a popular text at Qumran, both for its emphasis on "wilderness" and the moral life that must precede the coming of God. It is quoted in the Community Rule, followed by this interpretation: "This is the study of the law which he commanded through the hand of Moses, in order to act in compliance with all that has been revealed from age to age, and according to what the prophets have revealed through his holy spirit" (1QS 8:15–16). Individual qualities are spelled out in an allusion to the text in 1QS 4:1–2 (humility, patience, charity, goodness, understanding, trust, etc.), while separation from those who refuse to turn from wickedness is urged in 1QS 9:19–20. A rather different use occurs in the work known as *1 Enoch*, where the leveling of hills and valleys (Isa 40:4–5) is taken in an apocalyptic sense: "Mountains and high places will fall down and be frightened. And high hills shall be made low; and they shall melt like a honeycomb before the flame. And earth shall be rent asunder; and all that

17

is upon the earth shall perish" (1:6–7).[10] Thus like the Elijah texts, there was much expectation but little clarity as to what Isa 40:3 pointed towards. It was into this situation that John appeared in the wilderness, preaching his message of repentance.

WAS THE ROLE OF JOHN THE BAPTIST ACCORDING TO SCRIPTURE?

All four of the Gospels portray John as claiming to fulfill the words of Isa 40:3 and in Matthew and Luke, Jesus tells his disciples that John is the messenger of Mal 3:1. Interestingly, Mark does not have this saying but includes Mal 3:1 in his opening quotation, apparently attributing both to Isaiah:[11]

> The beginning of the good news of Jesus Christ, the Son of God. As it is written in the prophet Isaiah, "See, I am sending my messenger ahead of you, who will prepare your way; the voice of one crying out in the wilderness: 'Prepare the way of the Lord, make his paths straight,'" John the baptizer appeared in the wilderness, proclaiming a baptism of repentance for the forgiveness of sins.[12] (Mark 1:1–3)

On the other hand, while John's Gospel has John the Baptist identifying with Isa 40:3, he has him emphatically denying that he is the Messiah, Elijah, or the prophet (1:19–23). One could argue that Jesus' statements recorded in Matthew, Mark, and Luke come after John was executed and so John might not have been fully aware of his own role. However, a more likely solution concerns the nature of the claim itself. Luke 1:17 says that John will come "in the spirit and power of Elijah," not that he is the actual Elijah who lived some nine centuries earlier. After all, Luke records John's birth and speaks of his upbringing (1:80), so it is unlikely that he had the mature adult, thought to have been in the presence of God all these centuries, in mind. Indeed, it

10. Text from Charlesworth (ed.), *The Old Testament Pseudepigrapha*, I.13. *1 Enoch* is in fact a composite work and was very popular in the Qumran community.

11. Later scribes solved this by omitting the reference to Isaiah and using the plural "prophets." The two main solutions today are: (1) Mark wishes to assert that the "good news of Jesus Christ . . . is according to Isaiah" and hence the framework for understanding all the material; or (2) Mark is using a source that had already combined the two texts and uses Isaiah as the more prominent of the two prophets.

12. Most translations put a full stop after the quotation but the NRSV emphasizes John's ministry of baptism as its fulfillment. Joel Marcus (*Way of the Lord*, 12–47) thinks the comma should come after verse 1, so that it is the "good news of Jesus Christ" that is written in the prophet Isaiah.

is interesting that Luke omits both the discussion with the disciples about Elijah coming first and the question at the crucifixion of whether Elijah will come to save Jesus. Combined with the fact that Luke narrates a story where Jesus refers to the ancient Elijah as a precedent for his own ministry (4:25–26), it would seem that the question of John's fulfillment of the role of forerunner is primarily a christological one. If Jesus is the one who fulfills the expected coming of God, then John is the best candidate for the one who prepares his way, even if he was not fully aware of the role himself. Indeed, given his huge popularity, Luke's statement that he will come in the "spirit and power of Elijah" does not seem unreasonable.

Evidence for his huge popularity comes from both the New Testament and the Jewish historian, Josephus. Thus Mark speaks of the "*whole* Judean countryside and *all* the people of Jerusalem" going to be baptized (1:5). And in a debate about Jesus' identity, the leaders of Jerusalem are afraid to deny John's significance, "for *all* regarded John as truly a prophet" (11:32). Clearly this is exaggerated (technically known as hyperbole) but Josephus says much the same thing in his *Antiquities of the Jews,* where the crowds were drawn to John's preaching of "righteousness toward one another" and "piety toward God" and underwent a baptism "for purification." His popularity was such that Herod "feared lest the *great influence* John had over the people might put it into his power and inclination to raise a rebellion." So he had John executed and when some time later, Herod suffered defeat in a battle, the Jews believed that this was a punishment from God for what he had done to John.[13]

Nevertheless, there has been debate as to whether this popularity can reasonably be described as "restoring all things" (Mark 9:12). There are two ways one might answer this. The first is to see it in the light of the inaugurated fulfillment that is common to most of the claims made in the New Testament. Matthew says that Jesus will proclaim justice to the Gentiles and that they will find their hope in him (12:18), but this is hardly true of Jesus' earthly ministry, which was largely restricted to fellow Jews (15:24). Presumably Matthew had in mind the ministry to the Gentiles that would follow Jesus' death and resurrection (28:19–20). Similarly, John clearly did not "restore all things" on a global scale; his significance was limited to a very small part of what we now call the Middle East. But it was sufficient to prepare the way for Jesus, whose influence would ultimately be global.

13. *Antiquities* 18:116–19.

19

The second possibility is simply to note that the Hebrew text of Mal 4:5–6 does not speak of "restoring all things." This is a summary of the developing tradition rather than a quotation from a specific text. The disciples have heard the phrase from the scribes (Mark 9:11) and Jesus echoes it back to them, adding the comment: "But I tell you that Elijah has come, and they did to him whatever they pleased, as it is written about him" (9:13). It is not presented as the fulfillment of a specific text but the fulfillment of what was commonly thought about Elijah's return.

It is universally accepted that Jesus was baptized by John, for it was evidently a problem for the early church. In the first place, why would Jesus need to undergo a baptism for the forgiveness of sins? Developing understandings of atonement (2 Cor 5:21) required Jesus to be free from sin, so it is hardly something that the early church would invent. Second, it is customary for the junior person to be baptized by the senior, as can be seen from the rationalization that has crept into Matthew's account, where John is reported as saying: "I need to be baptized by you, and do you come to me?" (3:14). This allows Jesus to offer the explanation: "Let it be so now; for it is proper for us in this way to fulfill all righteousness" (3:15). Few scholars accept the authenticity of this dialogue but it does confirm the historicity of Jesus' baptism by John.

What of the claim that John is the voice of Isa 40:3? At first glance, it is clear from the Hebrew parallelism that Isaiah envisaged an actual journey through the wilderness so that the people could return to their homeland:

> A voice cries out:
> "*In the wilderness* prepare the way of the LORD,
> make straight *in the desert* a highway for our God." (Isa 40:3)

In the Gospels, the text is applied to John by changing the grammar of the sentence, so that it is the "voice" that is in the wilderness, rather than the "way" or "highway": "The voice of one crying out in the wilderness: 'Prepare the way of the Lord, make his paths straight'" (Luke 3:4). However, it is clear from what follows Isa 40:3 (and quoted in Luke 3:5–6) that the text also has an eschatological sense, for the result of this highway is that "the glory of the LORD shall be revealed, and *all people* shall see it together" (Isa 40:5). This can hardly refer to the actual journey through the wilderness, which was unlikely to be witnessed by anyone; it must therefore refer to what was to follow, namely, the rebuilding of Jerusalem and the future that awaits it. The Gospel writers see this fulfillment in the coming of Christ and all that will flow from it and they agree that the beginning of the gospel was the preparatory role of John (cf. Acts 10:37).

Can we be more specific about the use of Scripture here? It would seem that Isaiah had in mind the return of the exiles to Judea but the exalted language that follows suggests that he thought it would be the beginning of something much greater. It would be difficult to argue that he had an actual "forerunner" in mind but clearly some sort of "preparation" was envisaged before the prophecies could be realized. According to the Gospels, John fulfilled this role, preparing the way of God by calling Israel to repentance. It was a vision that attracted Jesus, as shown by his willingness to undergo baptism and it is possible that they spent some time working together (cf. John 3:22–26).

On the other hand, it would appear that John also entertained doubts about his role (Luke 7:9), perhaps because he was languishing in prison or perhaps because Jesus was not continuing to preach a message of repentance and judgment. Some scholars find this enquiry from John highly improbable and suggest that it is simply a literary device that allows Luke to proclaim that Jesus fulfilled the messianic signs from Isaiah.[14] However, it is surely unlikely that the early church would invent a story where such a popular prophet as John voices his doubts about Jesus, especially as Luke does not tell us whether John was convinced by Jesus' reply. In any event, whether John realized it or not, he clearly had some sort of preparatory role for Jesus, a figure who would eventually be revered by several billion people. It does not seem unreasonable, therefore, to suggest that John's preparatory role is at least a possible interpretation of Isa 40:3, particularly in the light of the verses that follow ("the glory of the LORD shall be revealed, and all people shall see it together").

There is an alternative view. Bishop Spong thinks that the idea of John as the forerunner of Jesus is a fabrication of the early church.[15] Acts 19:1–7 shows that not all of John's disciples became followers of Christ and the presence of a group in Ephesus indicates that they also had missionary ambitions. Luke's answer in this narrative is that they must be baptized in

---

14. "As if Herod Antipas would have granted his prisoner the leisure and liberty to discuss messianic claims" (Chilton, *Rabbi Jesus*, 63). Maurice Casey doubts the historicity of the setting but argues for the authenticity of the dialogue (Casey, *An Aramaic Approach to Q*, 105–45). It has often been stated that there is no evidence for the expectation that the Messiah would perform miracles but the discovery of the Qumran document 4Q521 has now changed this.

15. Spong, *Born of a Woman*, 114–15.

the name of the Lord Jesus and receive the Holy Spirit. In so doing, Luke continues a theme already found in Mark's Gospel that John's role was preparatory. He then extended it by including birth narratives where Jesus' superiority is emphasized at every point. John's Gospel, which is probably a decade or so later than Luke, goes even further by putting these words into John's mouth:

> No one can receive anything except what has been given from heaven. You yourselves are my witnesses that I said, "I am not the Messiah, but I have been sent ahead of him." He who has the bride is the bridegroom. The friend of the bridegroom, who stands and hears him, rejoices greatly at the bridegroom's voice. For this reason my joy has been fulfilled. He must increase, but I must decrease. (John 3:27–30)

Spong is clearly correct that later writers went out of their way to emphasize the subordination of John to Jesus but were they building on a tradition or inventing *de novo*? If the latter, then we must suppose that John's reputation for preaching and baptizing in the wilderness, along with the desire to present John's role as preparatory, led the early church to put the words of Isa 40:3 into his mouth. This then led to the words of Mal 3:1, a text which also speaks of "preparing the way," being put into Jesus' mouth and thus creating the tradition that associated John the Baptist with Elijah (cf. Mal 4:5–6). It is not impossible but to my mind, two things speak against it. First, if the catalyst in the discovery of Isa 40:3 was the word "wilderness," it is odd that the grammar of the text had to be altered to avoid the implication that the early church should be a "wilderness" community. It seems more likely that John thought of himself as preparing people in the wilderness for the coming of God, which the early church reinterpreted to fit its own circumstances. Second, if all of these traditions are the result of pure invention, it is strange that so many of them are ambiguous. One would have expected clear statements that John thought of himself as the returning Elijah whose role was to prepare the way for Jesus.

WAS JOHN'S INFANCY ACCORDING TO SCRIPTURE?

If it is agreed that John's preparatory role for Jesus is a plausible interpretation of Isa 40:3/Mal 3:1, this does not mean that the specific stories in Luke's infancy narrative are historically accurate. For example, there is no hint in any of the encounters between John and Jesus in the Gospels that they are related, and yet this is what is stated in the angelic message to Mary: "And now, your relative (*sungenis*) Elizabeth in her old age has also conceived a son" (Luke 1:36). Traditionally, John and Jesus are thought to be cousins, though the Greek word simply means "of the same kin." However, the difficulty is not so much their precise relationship but the suggestion that the two families were in close contact. How can this be reconciled with John 1:33, where it is said that John did not recognize Jesus until it was revealed to him, or the general tenure of the exchanges between them? It could be argued that Luke 1:80 says that John lived in the wilderness "until the day he appeared publicly to Israel," which would explain why they did not recognize one another when they eventually met as adults. However, most scholars regard the meeting between Elizabeth and Mary as contrived, and for our purposes it should be noted that it is not presented as a fulfillment of Scripture.[16]

Indeed, the only aspect of the birth of John that is specifically related to Scripture is the way that Luke uses the biblical theme of God overcoming barrenness to describe his conception. Can we say anything about the likelihood of this being the case? Clearly we are not in a position to say what God could or could not do but an argument in favor of its general historicity is the same as that put forward for Jesus' baptism. In recording the event, Luke comes perilously close to undermining the uniqueness of Jesus' birth, since John is also presented as a miracle child. Later tradition assumes that John was conceived through natural means, while Jesus was not, but the text does not actually say this:

> After those days his wife Elizabeth conceived, and for five months she remained in seclusion. She said, "This is what the Lord has done for me when he looked favorably on me and took away the disgrace I have endured among my people." (Luke 1:24–25)

> The angel said to her, "Do not be afraid, Mary, for you have found favor with God. And now, you will conceive in your womb and bear a son, and you will name him Jesus." (Luke 1:30–31)

In addition, Brown finds no convincing reason as to why Luke would invent the names of Zechariah and Elizabeth and concludes that much of the story was present in his sources.[17] Other scholars find this too "trusting"

16. Brown, *Birth of the Messiah*, 282–85. He notes that it was Wycliffe who popularized the view that John and Jesus were cousins.

17. Spong (*Born of a Woman*, 117–18) notes that the only other Elizabeth in Scripture is Elishiba, the wife of the first high priest Aaron (Exod 6:23). Is it more than coincidence,

of the narrative and suggest that it is more likely that "the sources" simply assumed that a prophet like John must have been a child of promise like Isaac, Samson, and Samuel. The idea that this would conflict with the significance of Jesus' birth can be answered in two ways. First, it could have come from disciples of John who were not influenced by Christianity. Second, it could have come from Christians who were in no doubt that Jesus was superior to John, and so any enhancement of John would correspondingly be an enhancement of Jesus. We will discuss this in more detail when we look at the birth of Jesus in chapter 5 but for the moment, since Luke is our only source for Zechariah and Elizabeth, the question must remain open.

CONCLUSION

The lack of clarity concerning Elijah's return and the nature of the "way" in the wilderness means that it is impossible to declare that Scripture unequivocally points to a particular forerunner for Jesus. We must therefore approach the question in a different way. Texts such as Mal 3:1, 4:5–6, and Isa 40:3 envisage a time of preparation before the coming of God, and associated with this are such things as a messenger, Elijah's return, and a way through the wilderness, which was understood in Jesus' day as a "way of life." If Jesus is understood as the fulfillment of the promised coming of God, either from the Gospel record or the world-wide movement that followed, then the claim that John was the one who prepared his way is quite plausible. It is likely that the sources relating to John have been embellished, particularly in terms of Mary and Elizabeth being related and perhaps also Elizabeth conceiving in her old age, but it is unlikely that the whole story was created *de novo*. We know from Josephus, as well as the New Testament, that John was widely regarded as a prophet and even if he himself was not always clear about his role, it is certain that he was a major influence on Jesus. Luke's statement about John coming in the "spirit and power of Elijah" (1:17) does not seem unduly exaggerated in the light of his great popularity and (more importantly) what followed. We cannot speak of Scripture "predicting" a forerunner for Jesus but John's preparatory role is at least a plausible interpretation/ application of texts like Mal 3:1, 4:5–6, and Isa 40:3.

---

he asks, that Aaron had a sister called Miriam, the Hebrew form of Mary?

2

Son of David

INTRODUCTION

MATTHEW OPENS HIS GOSPEL with the following declaration: "An account of the genealogy of Jesus the Messiah, the son of David, the son of Abraham" (1:1). This is followed by a set of names, which either Matthew or his source have organized into three sets of fourteens: "So all the generations from Abraham to David are fourteen generations; and from David to the deportation to Babylon, fourteen generations; and from the deportation to Babylon to the Messiah, fourteen generations" (1:17).[1] If the names are compared with the genealogies found in 1 Chr 1–9, it can been seen that Matthew has had to skip some generations to keep the number to fourteen[2] and most scholars think that the importance of the number is because it is the numerical value of the name David. In many ancient cultures, the letters of the alphabet were associated with particular numbers (a–1, b–2, etc.) and so a personal name has a particular value—a practice known as *gematria*. The best known example of this in the New Testament is found in Rev 13:8, where readers are invited to consider the number of the beast, which is given as 666. Most scholars think

1. Though oddly there are only thirteen names from the exile (Salathiel) to Jesus. Explanations for this have ranged from counting Jesus twice (his first and second coming), including Mary along with Joseph, counting David as both the end of the first fourteen and the beginning of the second or simply that a name has dropped out.

2. Matthew only lists Uzziah between Joram and Jotham (1:8–9) but 1 Chr 3:10–12 has four names (Ahaziah, Joash, Amaziah, Azariah). Since Azariah appears to be another name for Uzziah (2 Kgs 15:1–2; 2 Chr 26:3), it would seem that Matthew has omitted the first three names in order to obtain his fourteen generations.

this stands for Nero Caesar (written in Hebrew), a well-known persecutor of the church. The name David, in Hebrew, consists of three consonants: d (4), w (6), d (4), making a total of fourteen.[3]

The theme is reinforced when the angel appears to Joseph in a dream and says, "Joseph, son of David, do not be afraid to take Mary as your wife, for the child conceived in her is from the Holy Spirit" (1:20). This is slightly puzzling because Matthew wants to assert that Jesus was a "son of David" because Joseph was a "son of David" but then denies that Joseph was his biological father. We must presume that he regarded Joseph as Jesus' legal father and this was sufficient to support his case. There is a further reference when "wise men from the East"[4] came to Jerusalem and asked: "Where is the child who has been born king of the Jews? For we observed his star at its rising, and have come to pay him homage" (2:2). Although this does not mention David by name, the epithet "King of the Jews" corresponds to the "King David" in the genealogy (1:6) and this seems to be in deliberate opposition to what is said about "King Herod." Matthew is claiming that Jesus is the true successor of King David, not the upstart Herod.

Luke does not divide his genealogy into fourteens and it differs considerably from that of Matthew. Thus instead of beginning with Abraham and working forward to Jesus, he begins with Jesus and works back to Abraham and then back to Adam. He traces the line from Jesus to David via his son Nathan (a prophet) rather than Solomon (a king) and includes far more names than Matthew (fifty-seven from Abraham to Jesus compared with Matthew's forty-one). Luke does focus on David in other ways, however. Thus the angel Gabriel declares to Mary that God will give her son the "throne of his ancestor David" and he will "reign over the house of Jacob forever, and of his kingdom there will be no end" (1:32–33). Zechariah's prophecy includes the words, "He has raised up a mighty savior for us in the house of his servant David" (1:69) and a reason is given for why Jesus was born in Bethlehem: it was the "city of David." This is reiterated when the angel says to the shepherds, "to you is born this day in the city of David a Savior, who is the Messiah, the Lord" (2:11).

3. Ancient Hebrew texts consisted only of consonants. The vowel signs d^aw^id (hence David in English) were only added later. Alternatively, it may be that Matthew observed that there are fourteen generations between Abraham and David and wished to make a theological point that the same is true between David and the exile and the exile and Jesus.

4. The Greek word is *magos*, which can mean "magician" (Acts 13:6, 8), though most translations render the plural "wise men" (NIV transliterates, Magi). Because they are said to have followed a star, some have thought of them as "astrologers."

Thus the birth narratives of Matthew and Luke make two claims concerning Jesus and David. First, he is a direct descendant of David and they seek to demonstrate this by providing a list of names through either Nathan (Luke) or Solomon (Matthew). Second, he is not just any "son of David" (like the other names in the lists) but the *promised* "Son of David," who will reign over Israel and whose kingdom will have no end (Luke 1:32–33). In this chapter, we will investigate whether these two claims can be substantiated. In order to do this, we will first look at the nature of the "Son of David" promise in Scripture and its interpretation in the first century. We will then try to discover if Jesus saw himself as this "Son of David" and if so, how he understood the term. We will then be in a position to evaluate the claim made in the birth narratives that Jesus was not only *a* "son of David" but *the* "Son of David."

THE PROMISE OF A FUTURE "SON OF DAVID" IN SCRIPTURE

The key text for establishing the hope of a future "Son of David" is 2 Sam 7:12–14. The immediate recipient of the promise is clearly Solomon, since it speaks of building a house for God, but the words, "I will establish the throne of his kingdom *forever*," point beyond him:

> When your days are fulfilled and you lie down with your ancestors, I will raise up your offspring (*sperma*) after you, who shall come forth from your body, and I will establish his kingdom. He shall build a house for my name, and I will establish the throne of his kingdom forever. I will be a father to him, and he shall be a son to me. (2 Sam 7:12–14a)

This promise of a special relationship with God is echoed in the so-called royal psalms. Thus in Ps 45:7, the king is addressed with the words, "your God, has anointed you with the oil of gladness beyond your companions," and in Ps 2:7, "You are my son; today I have begotten you." Psalm 89 focuses on the enduring nature of the relationship, where his "line shall continue forever, and his throne endure before me like the sun" (89:36). However, what acted as a catalyst for the hope of a future "Son of David" were the extravagant claims made for this kingship: "Ask of me, and I will make the *nations* your heritage, and the *ends of the earth* your possession" (Ps 2:8). This was clearly not realized in David or Solomon and in the centuries that followed, far from ruling over the nations, Israel was subject to a succession of foreign powers. Thus prophets like Isaiah began to look forward to a future "Son of David" where the epithets would apply:

> A shoot shall come out from the stump of Jesse [David's father], and a branch shall grow out of his roots. The spirit of the LORD shall rest on him, the spirit of wisdom and understanding, the spirit of counsel and might, the spirit of knowledge and the fear of the LORD. His delight shall be in the fear of the LORD. He shall not judge by what his eyes see, or decide by what his ears hear; but with righteousness he shall judge the poor, and decide with equity for the meek of the earth. . . . On that day the root of Jesse shall stand as a signal to the peoples; the nations shall inquire of him, and his dwelling shall be glorious. (Isa 11:1–4, 10)

This spirit-filled person who will bring "equity for the meek of the earth" appears in the later chapters of Isaiah, where the setting has changed from the threat of Assyrian invasion in the eighth century BCE to the return from Babylon in the sixth century BCE.[5] This event seems to have sparked the hope that the promises would soon be realized: "Here is my servant, whom I uphold, my chosen, in whom my soul delights; I have put my spirit upon him; he will bring forth justice to the nations" (42:1). Indeed, in Isa 61:1 the promise is delivered in the first person: "The spirit of the Lord God is *upon me*, because the Lord has anointed *me*; he has sent *me* to bring good news to the oppressed, to bind up the brokenhearted, to proclaim liberty to the captives, and release to the prisoners." This could mean that the prophet thought these promises were being fulfilled in himself[6] or that his prophetic gift was to speak in the name of a future figure. Jeremiah had a similar hope:

> The days are surely coming, says the LORD, when I will raise up for David a righteous Branch, and he shall reign as king and deal wisely, and shall execute justice and righteousness in the land. In his days Judah will be saved and Israel will live in safety. And this is the name by which he will be called: "The LORD is our righteousness." (Jer 23:5–6)

5. It used to be thought that the Isaiah of the eighth century BCE was predicting events in the sixth century BCE but this is not how it reads. Rather, it sound like there was an actual prophet in the sixth century BCE delivering these words to the exiles. See Stromberg, *Introduction to the Study of Isaiah*, 1–54.

6. In the story of Philip's encounter with the Ethiopian eunuch, we are told that the man was reading the words of Isa 53:7–8 and then asked Philip: "About whom, may I ask you, does the prophet say this, about himself or about someone else?" (Acts 8:34).

Once the exiles had returned from Babylon and the temple had been re-built, the prophets Haggai and Zechariah focused their hopes on Joshua the high priest and Zerubbabel the governor. They were referred to as the "two anointed ones who stand by the Lord of the whole earth" (Zech 4:14) and Zerubbabel was even called, "my servant the Branch" (Zech 3:8) and lik-ened to a "signet ring," because God had chosen him (Hag 2:23). However, it did not amount to much and so the hopes were once again projected into the future. As we saw in the last chapter, Malachi envisaged a "messenger" who would prepare the way (3:1a), a "Lord" who would suddenly come to his temple (3:1b) and the prophet Elijah who would come "before the great and terrible day of the Lord" (4:5).

THE EXPECTATION OF A "SON OF DAVID" IN THE FIRST CENTURY

It has to be said that evidence for a coming "Son of David" in the first cen-tury is somewhat sparse. The only clear references are in *Psalms of Solomon* 17, four fragmentary documents found at Qumran, and a work variously known as *4 Esdras* (Vulgate), *2 Esdras* (KJV), or more commonly in English, *4 Ezra*. Since many other titles and phrases are used to express Israel's hopes (prince, scepter, star, elect or chosen one, anointed one, righteous one, Son of man, Son of God), there does not appear to be a particular focus on a Davidic figure.[7] However, William Horbury believes that this way of stating the matter is misleading, for it is more the case that these other titles and expressions have been drawn into the orbit of the royal promises. He notes that this tendency can already be seen in the editing of the biblical docu-ments and in some of the translation choices of the LXX. For example, the way that the birth of Judah's son Perez (Gen 38) interrupts the Joseph nar-rative reflects the fact that he was a forefather of David. The LXX rendering of the last phrase of Ps 110:3 ("From the womb of the morning, like dew, *your youth will come to you*") as "I have begotten you" makes a connection with Ps 2:7 ("You are my son; today I have begotten you") and the "scepter" of Gen 49:10 has become a "ruler."[8] This is an important observation and it alerts us to the possibility that the "Son of David" theme is not necessarily restricted to those passages where David is explicitly mentioned. On the other hand, by linking "Son of David" with these other titles and expres-

7. See Bird, *Are You the One Who is to Come?*, 31–62.

8. Horbury, *Jewish Messianism*, 36–63.

29

sions, the royal focus becomes somewhat blurred. That is why these six texts have played an important role in the discussion.

In the work known as the *Psalms of Solomon*, written in the first century B.C.E. and included in the LXX manuscripts that have come down to us, we read:

> See, O Lord, and raise up for them their king, the son of David, at the time which you choose, O God, to rule over Israel your servant. And gird him with strength to shatter in pieces unrighteous rulers. . . . [H]e shall gather a holy people whom he shall lead in righteousness. . . . He shall judge peoples and nations in the wisdom of his righteousness . . . for God has made him strong in the holy spirit and wise in the counsel of understanding. . . . And he shall lead all of them in equity . . . (*Pss. Sol.* 17:21, 22, 26, 29, 37, 41 NETS[9]).

In the Qumran literature, the text known as 4Q174 brings together the hope of a "Son of David" from 2 Sam 7:10–14 with the "branch of David" from Isa 11:1 and the "booth of David" from Amos 9:11 (also quoted in Acts 15:16). This figure will "arise with the Interpreter of the law [to rule] in Zion [at the end] of time . . . to save Israel" (I,11).[10] Two messianic figures are envisaged in this fragment, the promised "Son of David" and the "Interpreter of the law," which was perhaps inspired by Zerubbabel and Joshua (and earlier, Moses and Aaron). After further quotations from Ps 1:1, Isa 8:11, and Ezek 44:10, Ps 2:1 is quoted ("Why do the nations rage . . . against the Lord and his anointed?"), which is then applied to a future battle between the "kings of the nations" and "the elect of Israel in the last days" (I.19).[11]

A commentary on Gen 49:10 interprets the promise that a "scepter [shall not] depart from the tribe of Judah" as "there shall [not] fail to be a descendant of David upon the throne . . . until the Messiah of Righteousness comes, the Branch of David" (4Q252 fr. 5). David himself was of the tribe of Judah (1 Chr 2:4–15) and this text envisages a continuous line of

---

9. Quotations from the LXX are taken from Pietersma and Wright (eds.), *New English Translation of the Septuagint.*

10. Words in square brackets are where the text has been reconstructed because there is a gap in the manuscript or it is unreadable. Since we know how many letters are missing, this is usually a good guess, although scholars do sometimes differ in their suggestions. The 4Q stands for the fact that it was discovered in cave 4 and the I in the reference refers to column 1. In the texts quoted below, fr. stands for fragment.

11. Quotations from the Dead Sea Scrolls are taken from Vermes, *The Complete Dead Sea Scrolls.*

"sons of David" until the "branch of David" (Isa 11:1) comes, who is here called the "Messiah of Righteousness" (cf. Jer 23:6). This might explain the motive behind Matthew's genealogy, which provides a list of "sons of David" up to "Joseph the husband of Mary, of whom Jesus was born, *who is called the Messiah*" (Matt 1:16).

A commentary on Isa 11:1–3 interprets the "Branch of David" as one who will "arise at the end [of days]. . . . God will uphold him with [the spirit of might, and will give him] a throne of glory. . . . [He will put a scepter] in his hand and he shall rule over all the [nations]" (4Q161 fr. 8–10). Further comment on Isa 11:1–3 is found in 4Q285 fr. 7, where the "Branch of David" is identified with the "Prince of the Congregation," whose role is to judge and apparently to kill the leader of those opposing Israel (probably the Romans).[12]

Lastly, the book which we shall call *4 Ezra* (it is in fact a composite work) was written as a response to the fall of Jerusalem (70 C.E.), probably a few decades later. It draws on Daniel's visions to describe the persecution of God's people using the image of a great eagle. The pertinent text comes in chapter 12, which describes a lion who will "set free the remnant of my people, those who have been saved throughout my borders, and he will make them joyful until the end comes" (12:34 NRSV Apocrypha). As for the persecutors, he will "denounce them for their ungodliness and for their wickedness[;] . . . he will bring them alive before his judgment seat, and when he has reproved them, then he will destroy them" (12:33). The lion is identified as the "Messiah whom the Most High has kept until the end of days, who will arise from the offspring of David" (12:32). This is an intriguing verse since it appears to combine the traditional "Son of David" hope with the view that the Messiah remains in heaven until he is revealed in the last days. It is possible that the author has been influenced by the stories of Enoch and Elijah and envisages a returning "Son of David" rather than a figure yet to be born, or perhaps he simply did not notice the tension between these two ideas.

As noted above, it would be risky to deduce from just six texts that this is what Jews of the first century believed about the "Son of David," especially as the writings of Qumran represent a sectarian community. Nevertheless,

---

12. The text is fragmentary with many gaps. Vermes reconstructs as follows: "And there shall come forth a shoot from the stump of Jesse [. . .] the Branch of David and they will enter into judgement with [. . .] and the Prince of the Congregation, the Br[anch of David] will kill him [. . . by strok]es and by wounds. And a Priest [of renown(?)] will command [. . . the s]lai[n] of the Kitti[m . . .]."

it does show that *some* Jews continued to cherish hopes of a future "Son of David," who would reign over Israel and defeat all her enemies. Indeed, the nature of this defeat is described with some gusto in *Psalms of Solomon* 17 ("shatter in pieces unrighteous rulers") and 4Q285 even speaks of killing "[by strok]es and wounds." It is not surprising, therefore, that it is a matter of debate as to whether Jesus identified with such a figure or not.

DID JESUS CLAIM TO BE THE "SON OF DAVID"?

As with much in Mark's Gospel, the question of whether Jesus thought of himself as the promised "Son of David" is ambiguous. There are three stories to consider. The first is when a blind man called Bartimaeus cries out, "Jesus, Son of David, have mercy on me!" (10:47). Jesus does have mercy on him and declares: "Go; your faith has made you well" (10:52). However, it is unclear if the faith in question is the man's belief that Jesus is able to heal him or his statement that he is "Son of David." In favor of the former is the fact that Jesus specifically asks the man what he wants to happen and he replies, "My teacher [rabbi], let me see again" (10:51). On the other hand, Mark tells us that many were trying to prevent the man calling out to Jesus and so the request is repeated, including the "Son of David" phrase (10:48). Whichever is the case, there is no verbal confirmation from Jesus that he accepts the title.

The second story is when Jesus enters Jerusalem on a donkey and his followers shout out: "Hosanna! Blessed is the one who comes in the name of the Lord! Blessed is the coming kingdom of our ancestor David! Hosanna in the highest heaven!" (11:9–10). The actual title "Son of David" is not used but a close connection is established between Jesus' entry into Jerusalem and the coming kingdom of David. It is probable that Mark intends this as a true affirmation, but like the story of Peter's confession in Mark 8:29 ("You are the Messiah"), it is unclear if Jesus accepts the crowd's understanding of the term. His teaching that he came "not to be served but to serve" (10:45) is clearly at odds with the understanding of "Son of David" found in most of the documents discussed above and his entry on a donkey (perhaps to fulfill Zech 9:9) points to a humble king rather than a conquering Messiah. Certainly the events that follow suggest that the crowd's expectations were seriously mistaken.

The third story is initiated by Jesus himself. Citing the words of Ps 110:1, Jesus poses a riddle: "How can the scribes say that the Messiah is the

Son of David" when "David himself calls him Lord"? (Mark 12:35b, 37a). Most scholars agree that Jesus is not intending to deny that the Messiah is a descendant of David but is challenging the authority of the scribes. In other words, since Ps 110:1 contains such an obvious paradox, why is it that the scribes have not explained this to you? The reaction of the crowd is that they were "listening to him with delight" (12:37). Writing after the resurrection and ascension, it is probable that Mark understands Jesus' words as a veiled claim to be David's Lord (as Messiah) and David's son (as a descendant) but it is far from clear that this was Jesus' meaning. If it was, he clearly had a very different understanding of the role than what either the crowds or the scribes believed.

Luke has no additional stories but there are three more in Matthew where the title is used. The first is very similar to the story of Bartimaeus but occurs much earlier in the ministry. Two blind men come to Jesus and say, "Have mercy on us, Son of David!" (9:27). Jesus replies with a question, "Do you believe that I am able to do this?" (9:28) and when they answer in the affirmative, he says, "According to your faith let it be done to you" (9:29). As with the story of Bartimaeus, the status of the acclamation is left open.

The second story is in Matt 12:22–24, where the healing of a demoniac leads the crowd to ask, "Can this be the Son of David?" Since Matthew cites a contrary opinion, namely, that Jesus' power comes from "Beelzebul, the ruler of the demons" (12:24) it is clear in this instance that Matthew thinks the "Son of David" affirmation is correct, just as he makes clear in Matt 16:17–19 that Peter's confession that Jesus is the Messiah is correct.[13] However, there is no indication in the story that Jesus wishes to answer their question, either by affirming that he is the promised "Son of David" or by offering a reinterpretation of the role.

The third story concerns the healing of a Canaanite woman's daughter, which is the equivalent of Mark's story of the Syrophoenician woman's daughter. Mark reports her request for help in the third person (7:25) but Matthew includes the specific words: "Have mercy on me, Lord, Son of David; my daughter is tormented by a demon" (15:22). If it is true that

---

13. In Mark, Jesus does not acknowledge Peter's words and the rebuke that follows in 8:33 ("Get behind me, Satan! For you are setting your mind not on divine things but on human things") suggests that Peter's understanding is seriously deficient. Matthew also records this rebuke but not before Jesus has accepted Peter's affirmation with the words: "Blessed are you, Simon son of Jonah! For flesh and blood has not revealed this to you, but my Father in heaven" (16:17).

Matthew has taken this story from Mark, as most scholars believe,[14] then the christological titles appear to be Matthew's own addition, just as he introduces the title "Son of God" into the stilling of the storm episode (Matt 14:33/Mark 6:51–52) and Peter's confession (Matt 16:16/Mark 8:29). Clearly Matthew believes that Jesus is the expected "Son of David" but he knows of no stories or sayings where Jesus actually affirms it. In this story, the woman's persistence prompts Jesus to claim that he was "sent only to the lost sheep of the house of Israel" (15:24), which could perhaps be taken to mean something like: "You call me Son of David so why are you, a foreigner, asking for my help?" But her replies ("Lord help me" and "Yes, Lord, yet even the dogs eat the crumbs that fall from their master's table") suggest the emphasis lies elsewhere. In any case, as with the rest of the stories, Jesus neither accepts nor denies the title.[15]

The only other example in the Gospels comes in John 7. Most scholars think that John's Gospel was written towards the end of the first century and so its witness to Jesus' words is often treated with suspicion. However, for our purposes, it is not so much the actual dialogue that is important but the author's desire to show that there were diverse views concerning the identity of Jesus. Thus some were asking:

> Can it be that the authorities really know that this is the Messiah? Yet we know where this man is from; but when the Messiah comes, no one will know where he is from. . . . On the last day of the festival, the great day, while Jesus was standing there, he cried out, "Let anyone who is thirsty come to me, and let the one who believes in me drink." . . . When they heard these words, some in the crowd said, "This is really the prophet." Others said, "This is the Messiah." But some asked, "Surely the Messiah does not come from Galilee, does he? Has not the scripture said that the Messiah is descended from David and comes from Bethlehem, the village where David lived?" So there was a division in the crowd because of him. (John 7:26–27, 37–38, 40–43)

Since irony is a well-known feature of John's Gospel (cf. 11:50; 18:14), it is possible that the author expects his readers to know the stories of Jesus'

---

14. The reasons for this are set out in most introductions to the New Testament, for example, Ehrman, *The New Testament*; Puskas and Crump, *Introduction to the Gospels and Acts*.

15. Since Jesus does eventually agree to her request, one could argue that he is challenging her to rethink her understanding of the title but this seems overly subtle.

birth in Bethlehem, even though he does not include them in his gospel.[16] The crowd would then be inadvertent witnesses to the claim that Jesus was the Messiah, the Son of David, because he was not only the bearer of the Spirit (Isa 42:1; 61:1) but was also born in Bethlehem (Mic 5:2). On the other hand, the passage also notes that some believed that "when the Messiah comes, no one will know where he is from," probably a reference to the view found in *4 Ezra* that the Messiah remains in heaven until he is revealed in the last days. We will discuss the question of whether Jesus was in fact born in Bethlehem in the next chapter but for now, we simply note that the author of John's Gospel thinks that there was a variety of views in the first century concerning the promised "Son of David."

In summary, the Gospels show that not only was there considerable ambiguity as to the meaning of the title "Son of David" in the first century, there is very little evidence that Jesus actually identified with such a figure. This is not surprising given the traditions of military conquest found in texts like *Psalms of Solomon* 17 and 4Q285. The debate probably comes down to a choice between one of the following statements: (1) Jesus saw himself as the promised "Son of David" but did not wish to proclaim it because his understanding of the role was very different from popular conceptions; or (2) The church came to believe that Jesus was the Messiah and so *assumed* that Jesus must have understood himself to be the promised "Son of David." Interestingly, advocates of both positions make appeal to what is found in the rest of the New Testament.

THE "SON OF DAVID" IN THE REST OF THE NEW TESTAMENT

In the New Testament, the claim that Jesus is the promised "Son of David" is confined to a few passages in Paul (Rom 1:3; 15:12; 2 Tim 2:8), Acts (13:23; 15:16) and Revelation (3:7; 5:5; 22:16). Paul begins his letter to the Romans by claiming that Jesus was "descended from David according to the flesh and was declared to be Son of God with power according to the spirit of holiness by resurrection from the dead" (1:3–4). This verse has given rise to

---

16. The same could be said for the last supper traditions. John does not include the particular words over the bread and wine ("This is my body . . . This is my blood") but in the discourse that follows the feeding of the 5,000, he has Jesus say: "Those who eat my flesh and drink my blood have eternal life, and I will raise them up on the last day; for my flesh is true food and my blood is true drink" (John 6:54–55).

much debate, especially the precise meaning of the word translated here as "declared" (*horisthentos*). Is Paul saying that Jesus was an ordinary descendant of David (like Joseph) but became something else ("Son of God") at his resurrection? In favor of this, one could cite Paul's only reference to the birth of Jesus in all of his writings:

> But when the fullness of time had come, God sent his Son, *born of a woman, born under the law,* in order to redeem those who were under the law, so that we might receive adoption as children. (Gal 4:4–5)

The thrust of this verse appears to be that Jesus was born under the same conditions as the rest of humanity and that is why humanity can be redeemed. As we shall see later, this has implications for the question of whether Paul believed in the virginal conception of Jesus, for that would surely make him very different from the rest of humanity. On the other hand, Paul says that "God sent his Son," suggesting that he bore this title before the resurrection, indeed before his birth.[17] If this is the case, then the two phrases might not be intended as a contrast (born human but of divine origin) but both used to support the view that Jesus fulfills the scriptural promises: Not only is he the "Son of God," as demonstrated by the resurrection, he is also a descendant of David, as promised in texts like 2 Sam 7:14.

Later in the letter, Paul strings together a number of quotations to the effect that it has always been God's intention to include Gentiles into the people of God (15:9–12). The final quotation is from Isa 11:10, which Paul quotes in the form: "The root of Jesse shall come, the one who rises to rule the Gentiles; in him the Gentiles shall hope" (15:12).[18] Although the emphasis is on the inclusion of the Gentiles, Paul feels no need to defend the assertion that Jesus is the promised "root of Jesse," even to a church that he has never visited. Along with the evidence of Rom 1:3–4, it would appear that it was the common belief of the early church that Jesus was not only a descendant of David but *the* promised "Son of David."

Interestingly, the only other reference in the Pauline corpus occurs in 2 Tim 2:8, where we have the same juxtaposition: "Remember Jesus Christ, raised from the dead, a descendant of David—that is my gospel" (2 Tim

17. On the other hand, John 1:6 can talk of God sending John the Baptist but the implication is not that John is pre-existent.

18. Paul is here following the LXX, which differs considerably from the Hebrew text: "On that day the root of Jesse shall *stand as a signal* to the peoples; the nations shall *inquire* of him, and his dwelling shall be glorious" (Isa 11:10 NRSV).

36

2:8). Some scholars think that the letters to Timothy and Titus (known as the Pastoral Epistles) were not written directly by Paul (the style and vocabulary are very different) but by a later disciple, perhaps using notes smuggled out of prison. If this is the case, then 2 Tim 2:8 looks like a summary of Rom 1:3–4 and tells us nothing further about Paul's thought. On the other hand, other scholars think the differences between the Pastoral Epistles and letters like 1 and 2 Corinthians, Romans, and Galatians can be satisfactorily explained by the different situation: Paul is writing to individuals rather than churches and some ten to fifteen years later. Either way, it seems that Paul can assume that Jesus' descent from David is a commonplace but makes no attempt to draw out its theological significance.[19]

The name "David" is mentioned twelve times in Acts, mainly in his (assumed) prophetic role as speaking about the betrayal of Jesus (1:16), his mistreatment by the rulers (4:25), his resurrection (2:31; 13:34), his ascension (2:34), and the calling of the Gentiles (15:16–17). Two of the references are significant for our theme. The first occurs in Paul's sermon to the synagogue in Antioch. Paul is said to have quoted Ps 16 to the effect that David spoke of the resurrection of Jesus (as did Peter in Acts 2:31) but then added: "Of this man's posterity ("seed") God has brought to Israel a Savior, Jesus, as he promised" (13:23). The term "savior" (*soter*) does not occur very often in Scripture and when it does, it either refers to God (Isa 45:15) or one of Israel's deliverers/judges (Judg 3:9; Neh 9:27). It is never applied to a future figure in the Hebrew Bible but the LXX renders Isa 62:11 ("See, your salvation comes; *his* reward is with him, and his recompense before him") as "See, your savior comes to you." However, it does not appear that Paul is alluding to a specific verse; the descendant of David can be called "savior" because he will bring about the promised deliverance.[20] Since this is described as setting people free from their sins (13:39), it would appear to be closer to the traditions of Isa 11:1–4 ("equity for the meek of the earth") and 61:1 ("liberty to the captives") than the traditions of *Psalms of Solomon* and the Dead Sea Scrolls.

19. For the reasons why many scholars think the Pastoral Epistles do not come directly from Paul, see the relevant chapter in Ehrman, *The New Testament*.

20. See Zech 9:9 ("Lo, your king comes to you; triumphant and victorious is he, humble and riding on a donkey, on a colt, the foal of a donkey"), which is closely linked with Isa 62:11 by its address to "daughter Zion," and uses the participle of the verb "to save," which could be rendered "a saving person," that is, a savior. It should be noted that there is a debate as to whether these are Paul's words or Luke's construction of what someone like Paul would have said. See Moyise, *Later New Testament Writers and Scripture*, 6–41.

The other passage occurs during the so-called Jerusalem council in Acts 15. The topic of discussion is whether Gentile Christians need to be circumcised in order to belong to the people of God (15:1). Various people speak, including Peter, Paul, and Barnabas, before James cites Amos 9:11–12 as evidence that God's promises have always included Gentiles:

> After this I will return, and I will rebuild the dwelling of David, which has fallen; from its ruins I will rebuild it, and I will set it up, so that all other peoples may seek the Lord—even all the Gentiles over whom my name has been called. Thus says the Lord, who has been making these things known from long ago. (Acts 15:16–18)

There are a number of difficulties with this quotation[21] but for our purposes, the main question is to determine the meaning of the phrase, "dwelling of David." The double use of the word "rebuild" could suggest that the temple is in mind but at the time of Amos and the time envisaged by Acts (though not necessarily when Acts was written), the Jerusalem temple was still standing. Thus it is probably a reference to the restoration of the Davidic dynasty and hence the fulfillment of texts like 2 Sam 7:14 and Isa 11:1–4. James no doubt assumed that this came about through the death and resurrection of Jesus but that is not the purpose of the quotation and he does not elaborate. What it does tell us, along with Acts 13, is that the author of Acts thought that both Paul and James believed the promises made to David had been fulfilled in Jesus, even though Israel does not appear to have been delivered or her oppressors subdued. It is likely that they thought these promises had *begun* to be fulfilled in the Christian community.

In Revelation, Jesus is called the "key of David" (3:7) and the "root of David" (5:5) and the book ends with Jesus' own declaration: "It is I, Jesus, who sent my angel to you with this testimony for the churches. I am the root (*rhiza*) and the descendant (*genos*) of David, the bright morning star" (22:16). This is the only place in the New Testament where Jesus explicitly

---

21. The Hebrew text as translated in the NRSV reads: "On that day I will raise up the booth of David that is fallen, and repair its breaches, and raise up its ruins, and rebuild it as in the days of old; in order that they may *possess the remnant of Edom and all the nations* who are called by my name, says the LORD who does this." It would appear that the LXX translator took the consonants for the word "Edom" to be the word "Adam," so that the "remnant of Edom" has become "all other peoples," and was then made the subject of the sentence (they will seek) rather than the object (Israel will possess them). Many scholars find it unlikely that the historical James would have used the LXX in the middle of Jerusalem to make such a point and suggest that we are here reading Luke's theology. See Moyise, *Later New Testament Writers*, 11–12.

claims to be the "descendant of David" and it is possible that the two terms (*rhiza, genos*) are intended to encapsulate the scriptural hope: Jesus is both a "descendant" of David (2 Sam 7:14) and the promised "root" of David (Isa 11:1, 10). On the other hand, if this was John's intention, it is surprising that he does not use the Greek word *sperma* for "descendant," which is found in 2 Sam 7:12 and traditionally associated with such promises. It is true that *genos* can mean "descendant" (Acts 17:28) but it more generally means "race" (Mark 7:26; Acts 4:36; 1 Pet 2:9) or "kind" (Matt 13:47; Mark 9:29; 1 Cor 14:10) and is never associated with the Davidic promises in the LXX. Perhaps John is not thinking of specific passages but summarizing the scriptural hope of a future Davidic figure.[22]

The title "root of David" is also found in Rev 5:5, where one of the elders says to John: "See, the Lion of the tribe of Judah, the Root of David, has conquered, so that he can open the scroll and its seven seals." It is of interest that in Rev 5:5 and 22:16, John combines the title with a phrase that emphasizes conquest. In the latter it was "bright morning star," which derives from Num 24:17 ("a star shall come out of Jacob, and a scepter shall rise out of Israel; it shall crush the borderlands of Moab and the territory of all the Shethites"). In Rev 5:5, it is the "Lion of the tribe of Judah," which looks back to the promises made to Judah in Gen 49:9–10:

> Judah is a lion's whelp; from the prey, my son, you have gone up.
> He crouches down, he stretches out like a lion, like a lioness—who
> dares rouse him up? The scepter shall not depart from Judah, nor
> the ruler's staff from between his feet, until tribute comes to him;
> and the obedience of the peoples is his. (Gen 49:9–10)

Both texts are treated as messianic in later Jewish writings,[23] and it would appear that John wishes to keep the "conquest" motif uppermost, even though he believes the victory was won by Jesus on the cross (5.6, 12). The reference to the "key of David" is more complicated. It occurs in the message to the church in Philadelphia, where the speaker says to John: "These are the words of the holy one, the true one, who has the key of David, who opens and no one will shut, who shuts and no one opens" (3:7). The reference to "opening" and "closing" makes it certain that Isa 22:22 is in mind,

---

22. Sir 47:22 (included in the NRSV Apocrypha) uses the word *ekgonos* (which is approximately cognate with *genos*) for "descendant" in close connection with *sperma* ("seed") and *rhiza* ("root") and this could provide a precedent for John's usage.

23. *T. Levi* 18:3; 4QTest 9–13 ("morning star"); *T. Jud.* 24:5; *4 Ezra* 12:31–34 ("Lion of Judah").

a text where Eliakim is given the "key to the house of David" and will become a "throne of honor to his ancestral house" (22:23). It would appear that Eliakim's failure (Isa 22:25) has led to a messianic interpretation where Jesus holds the keys of the Davidic kingdom, just as he holds the keys to Death and Hades (Rev 1:18).[24]

In summary, the evidence of the New Testament is rather like that of the Dead Sea Scrolls. If the texts are quoted together, it is clear that the early church believed that Jesus was the promised "Son of David" but it is not a major theme. Indeed, given that the promised "Son of David" was thought to bring safety to Israel and Judah, administer justice and righteousness in the land, and remove the wicked (Jer 23:5; Isa 11:4), it is surprising that the New Testament authors do not seek to reinterpret or clarify its meaning. In the decades following Jesus' death, it is hardly obvious that such promises have been fulfilled or even begun to be fulfilled. This makes it likely that the tradition was associated with Jesus from the earliest times and was not invented at a later time to bolster the claims of Christianity.[25]

Did Jesus think of himself as the promised "Son of David"? Brown argues that if Jesus did not regard himself as "Son of David," there is nothing in Scripture that suggests that coming back to life would lead his disciples to that conclusion. The widow's son that Elijah brought back to life (1 Kgs 17:17–24) was not regarded as the promised "Son of David" and (presumably) nor were those brought back to life in the New Testament (Mark 5:38–43; Luke 7:12–15; John 11:1–45; Acts 9:37–41). He concludes that the most likely solution is that Jesus did think of himself as "Son of David" but did not openly proclaim it, because his view of the role was very different from the popular view.[26] On the other hand, the New Testament is full of texts that were used by the early church but cannot be traced back to Jesus. For example, Luke presents Peter and Paul using Ps 16 to show that David foresaw Jesus' resurrection, but there is no evidence that Jesus ever used this text.[27] What is perhaps worth saying is that had the Gospels presented

24. Beale (*Book of Revelation*, 284) argues that this is not simply an analogical use of Scripture but typological fulfillment, noting among other things the similarities with the messianic Isa 9:6–7 and the fact that Eliakim is called "my servant" in Isa 22:22.

25. Brown (*Birth of the Messiah*, 507) adds Heb 7:14 as evidence, since the author has to explain how Jesus can be our High Priest, given that he is descended from Judah (hence David) rather than Aaron.

26. Ibid., 505–12.

27. This can of course be countered by saying that this is one of the texts that Jesus taught the disciples in the period after the resurrection: "Then beginning with Moses and

Jesus as openly proclaiming his Davidic descent, many scholars would be even more suspicious that this was Jesus' view. The fact that the Gospels are ambiguous is perhaps a point in favor of Brown's position.

WAS JESUS DESCENDED FROM DAVID?

Ironically, the evidence presented above would probably lead us to accept that Jesus was a descendant of David (like Joseph) if it were not for the genealogies in Matthew and Luke, which claim to give the actual line of descendants. The problem, as we have already noted, is that the two genealogies appear to be contradictory. For our purposes, we can concentrate on two issues: (1) Matthew says that Joseph's father was called Jacob, Luke says it was Heli; (2) Matthew has eight names between Joseph's father and Zerubbabel, Luke has eighteen.

Matthew	Luke
Zerubbabel	*Zerubbabel*
Abiud	Rhesa, Joanan
Eliakim	Joda, Joeech
Azor	Semein, Mattathias
Zadok	Maath, Naggai
Achim	Esli, Nahum
Eliud	Amos, Mattathias, Joseph
Eleazar	Jannai, Melchi, Levi
Matthan	Matthat
Jacob	Heli
Joseph	*Joseph*
Jesus	*Jesus*

The simplest solution would be if Jacob and Heli were alternative names for the same person, especially as Matthan and Matthat might easily be variant spellings of his father's name. However, since there is no agreement on any of the other names between Zerubbabel and Matthan/Matthat, this would have to be true of everyone else, which is hardly likely. Most scholars, therefore, think that Jacob and Heli are different people and represent the legal and biological fathers of Joseph. This can be explained in two ways. First, if Jacob and Heli were brothers and the one married to Joseph's mother died, levirate law would require the surviving brother to marry her and

---

all the prophets, he interpreted to them the things about himself in all the Scriptures" (Luke 24:27).

41

"the firstborn whom she bears shall succeed to the name of the deceased brother, so that his name may not be blotted out of Israel" (Deut 25:6).[28] Once again, however, this simply moves the problem back through the generations: we must suppose that Eleazar and Levi (or Jannai/Melchi) are also brothers and at one time married to the mother of Matthan/Matthat, and so on. This explanation can safely be discounted.

The second explanation is that Matthew has given us the genealogy of Joseph, while Luke has given us the genealogy of Mary. There is a certain plausibility to this since it is well known that Matthew's infancy story focuses on Joseph (and his dreams), while Luke's focuses on Mary (annunciation, visit to Elizabeth, song of praise).[29] Given that both gospels claim that Joseph was not Jesus' biological father, it would not be surprising if one of them (Luke) took the unusual step of tracing the genealogy through his mother. Indeed, Luke introduces the genealogy with the words: "Jesus was about thirty years old when he began his work. He was the son (as was thought) of Joseph son of Heli" (3:23). On this theory then, the "as was thought" is an indicator that what follows is not the genealogy of Joseph but the genealogy of Mary. This is then justified by suggesting that Mary was an only child and so when she married Joseph, her father Heli adopted Joseph as his legal heir. This is more plausible than the first explanation but it does not explain why Luke has eighteen names between Zerubbabel and Jesus and Matthew only eight. Are we to assume that everyone in Mary's line died young and that is why there are twice as many fathers than in Joseph's line?

Lastly, we might mention that 1 Chr 3:19–20 makes no mention of Abiud (Matthew) or Rhesa (Luke) as among the sons of Zerubbabel and so along with the above, most scholars think that the genealogies serve a theological rather than a historical purpose. For example, when Matthew lists Joseph's father as Jacob, is he drawing our attention to the patriarch Jacob, who became the father of the twelve tribes of Israel? If so, then he may have had this verse in mind: "Now Israel[30] loved Joseph more than any other of his children, because he was the son of his old age" (Gen 37:3). Of course, it could be a coincidence that Joseph's father was called Jacob but

28. The first known reference to levirate marriage as an explanation comes from Julius Africanus (c. 225 CE), as recorded in Eusebius, *Eccl. Hist.* I:7.

29. One might also note that in the story of Jesus' rejection in his home town, Mark has the crowd asking, "Is not this the carpenter, *the son of Mary* . . . ?" (6:3) but this is eliminated in Matthew's version: "Is not this the *carpenter's son*? Is not his mother called Mary?" (13:55).

30. Jacob was renamed Israel in Gen 32:28.

it is interesting that dreams play an important part in Matthew's narrative (1:20–21; 2:13, 19, 22), just as they do in the stories of the biblical Joseph (Gen 37, 40–41).[31] Brown concludes:

> This means that, while the two NT genealogies tell us how to evaluate Jesus, they tell us nothing certain about his grandparents or his great grandparents. The message about Jesus, son of Joseph, is not that factually he is also (grand) son of either Jacob (Matthew) or of Eli (Luke) but that theologically he is "son of David, son of Abraham" (Matthew), and "Son of God" (Luke).[32]

CONCLUSION

It is clear that the early church believed Jesus to be the promised "Son of David," but with the exception of Matthew and Luke, there does not appear to be any interest in his actual forefathers, and even Joseph fades from view.[33] This raises the question of whether the genealogies of Matthew and Luke are primarily theological rather than historical. This is particularly so for Matthew, with his three groups of fourteen names, inclusion of five women (Tamar, Rahab, Ruth, Bathsheba, Mary), and evocative names from Israel's past, like Jacob and Zadok. On the other hand, most of the pre-exilic names agree with what we find in Scripture (generally with LXX spellings) and so by analogy, we might assume that they were doing something similar for the post-exilic period, namely, modifying and embellishing rather than creating and inventing. Certainty is impossible but Brown is probably not too far from the truth in stating that while there is some basis in history, the main point of the genealogies is theological.

This leaves us with the question of whether the theological claim that Jesus was the promised "Son of David" is credible. In the past, this has been argued in simplistic terms, as if Scripture points unequivocally to a single

31. Gundry (*Matthew*, 22) says: "The famous dreams of the patriarch Joseph (Gen 37:5–11) influenced Matthew to conform the traditional vision of Zechariah and visitation to Mary in the daytime (Luke 1:11, 22, 26–28, 38) to the OT pattern of Joseph's dreams in the nightime." It should be noted that Gundry thinks that Matthew had access to Luke's infancy narrative.

32. Brown, *Birth of the Messiah*, 94.

33. The only other reference outside of Matthew and Luke is John 1:45. A possible explanation is that Joseph died soon after Jesus' birth but it might also be that Jesus' physical descent was of no importance to the theological claims that were being made about him.

messianic figure and Jesus claimed to be that person. However, as we have seen, the reality is much more complicated, both in terms of the diversity of future hopes (and how they were understood in the first century) and the ambiguity of what Jesus actually claimed. For Crossan and Borg, the issue is whether Jesus stood for an alternative kingship to Caesar and his puppet king, Herod. It is not about the supposed superiority of Christianity over Judaism—a later Christian idea that is utterly anachronistic in a first-century context—but the battle between imperial domination and justice and righteousness. By common consent, Jesus taught another way and whenever human beings have put this into practice, the world has been changed for the better. Their conclusion is, I think, a fitting conclusion to this chapter:

> Jesus is not the fulfillment of miraculously specific predictions. Rather, he is the fulfillment of the Law and the Prophets in a much more comprehensive sense. . . . He is their crystallization, their expression in an embodied life. He decisively reveals and incarnates the passion of God as disclosed in the Law and the Prophets—the promise and hope for a very different kind of world from the world of Pharaoh and Caesar, the world of domination and empire.[34]

34. Crossan and Borg, *First Christmas*, 224.

44

3

Bethlehem and Nazareth

INTRODUCTION

THERE IS NOTHING CONTROVERSIAL about the claim that Jesus grew up in the Galilean town of Nazareth. In the Gospels, he is called "Jesus of Nazareth" by Bartimaeus (Mark 10:47), the guards (John 18:5), a servant girl (Matt 26:71), an angel (Mark 16:6), Cleopas (Luke 24:19), and even a demon (Luke 4:34). According to Mark, Jesus' public ministry began when he "came from Nazareth of Galilee and was baptized by John in the Jordan" (Mark 1:9). When he later returns to his hometown (*patris*), they take offense because his success is not in keeping with his humble origins: "Is not this the carpenter, the son of Mary and brother of James and Joses and Judas and Simon, and are not his sisters here with us?" (Mark 6:3). In John's Gospel, Philip says to Nathanael: "We have found him about whom Moses in the law and also the prophets wrote, Jesus son of Joseph from Nazareth" (John 1:45).[1] And according to Acts, it was a regular part of the preaching of the gospel (2:22; 3:6; 4:10; 10:38; 22:8; 26:9).

On the other hand, both Matthew and Luke report that Jesus was actually born in Bethlehem, a small town five or six miles south of Jerusalem. This is Luke's explanation for how this came about:

> In those days a decree went out from Emperor Augustus that all the world should be registered. This was the first registration and was taken while Quirinius was governor of Syria. All went to their

1. Prompting Nathanael's derisive reply: "Can anything good come out of Nazareth?" (John 1:46).

45

> own towns to be registered. Joseph also went from the town of Nazareth in Galilee to Judea, to the city of David called Bethlehem, because he was descended from the house and family of David. He went to be registered with Mary, to whom he was engaged and who was expecting a child. While they were there, the time came for her to deliver her child. (Luke 2:1–6)

Luke clearly envisages Joseph and Mary residing at Nazareth before the birth of Jesus (1:26) and returning to Nazareth when the requirements of the law had been fulfilled (2:39). Matthew, however, appears to think that Joseph and Mary lived in Bethlehem (2:11), fled to Egypt because of Herod's threats, and made their home in Nazareth only because Herod's successor, his brother Archelaus, was also a threat (2:22). In terms of the fulfillment of Scripture, Luke simply wishes to emphasize that Joseph was a descendant of David and that is why he had to return to Bethlehem. Matthew, however, provides specific quotations to support the statements that Jesus was born in Bethlehem but grew up in Nazareth:

> King Herod . . . inquired of them [chief priests and scribes] where the Messiah was to be born. They told him, "In Bethlehem of Judea; for so it has been written by the prophet: 'And you, Bethlehem, in the land of Judah, are by no means least among the rulers of Judah; for from you shall come a ruler who is to shepherd my people Israel.'" (Matt 2:3–6)

> But when he [Joseph] heard that Archelaus was ruling over Judea in place of his father Herod, he was afraid to go there. And after being warned in a dream, he went away to the district of Galilee. There he made his home in a town called Nazareth, so that what had been spoken through the prophets might be fulfilled, "He will be called a Nazorean." (Matt 2:22–23)

These quotations raise a number of questions. For example, if it was clear from Scripture that the Messiah would be born in Bethlehem, the story of the "guiding star" would appear to be redundant. As we will see below, the quotation comes from Mic 5:2[2] and far from claiming that Bethlehem is "*by no means* least among the rulers of Judah," it actually claims that it is the least.[3] Even more problematic is the second quotation, for the town of

2. In both the Hebrew text and the LXX, it is Mic 5:1, and this is followed by some English versions (NJB), but we will follow the numbering of the NRSV.

3. The Hebrew can mean "little" or "too little," hence RSV ("who are little"), NRSV ("who are one of the little"), NIV ("though you are small"), NJB ("the least"). The Greek word *oudamos* ("by no means") has been inserted into the quotation, either by Matthew

46

Nazareth is never mentioned in Israel's Scripture and the words, "He will be called a Nazorean," do not exist. It is of course possible that Matthew is quoting from a source that is no longer extant, but most scholars believe that he is offering a wordplay with either the *nazir* ("Nazirite") of Num 6:2, Judg 13:5, 7, and 1 Sam 1:11, or the *neser* ("branch") of Isa 11:1. Each of these suggestions might be important theologically—Jesus is either dedicated to God and holy (*nazir*) or the messianic branch (*neser*)—but hardly supports the contention that he had to come from Nazareth.

The more general issue is that Luke seems to think Mary and Joseph came from Nazareth and so provides a rationale for how Jesus came to be born in Bethlehem, while Matthew thinks they resided in Bethlehem and provides a rationale for how Jesus grew up in Nazareth. At first glance, Luke looks the better option since he does not appeal to a piece of "creative exegesis" but to public events. However, the only evidence of a census under Quirinius was in 6–7 C.E. and this only affected Judea, since Galilee was under the tetrarchy of Antipas at this time. Thus it is equally possible that Luke's explanation for the birth of Jesus in Bethlehem depends on a "creative" (or mistaken) account of the census. It is a conundrum that continues to baffle scholars and we will begin our study by looking at the quotation of Mic 5:2 and how it was understood in Jesus' day.

MICAH 5:2

The first thing to say about Matthew's quotation is that the final phrase ("who is to shepherd my people Israel") does not come from Micah but is taken from 2 Sam 5:2 (or the identical 1 Chr 11:2). Here, the people remind David that "the LORD said to you: It is you who shall be shepherd of my people Israel, you who shall be ruler over Israel." It is easy to see how a Jewish exegete would take Mic 5:2 and 2 Sam 5:2 as referring to the same person, especially as Micah goes on to say that the ruler from Bethlehem will "shepherd his flock in the strength of the LORD" (Mic 5:4, NIV). According to Matthew, Micah's promise of a ruler from Bethlehem was well known among the chief priests and scribes and John 7:42 suggests that it was well known among the people. If this is the case, then it is possible that the Evangelists "created" their stories in order to show that Jesus was born in Bethlehem, even though he was known as "Jesus of Nazareth." Before

---

or his source, presumably to highlight that now that the Messiah has been born, Bethlehem will no longer be regarded as insignificant.

47

we can evaluate this, we must first consider the meaning of Mic 5:2 and its interpretation in the first century. The NRSV (representing the Hebrew) and NETS (representing the Greek of the Septuagint) read as follows:

Mic 5:2 (NRSV)	Mic 5:2 (NETS)
But you, O Bethlehem of Ephrathah, who are one of the little clans of Judah, from you shall come forth for me one who is to rule in Israel, whose origin is from of old, from ancient days.	And you, O Bethleem, house of Ephratha, are very few in number to be among the thousands of Ioudas; one from you shall come forth for me to become a ruler (*archon*) in Israel, and his goings forth (*exodoi*) are from of old, from days of yore.

The Greek has taken the Hebrew word for "clans" literally and rendered it "thousands" and has changed the verb ("to *rule* in Israel") to a noun ("a *ruler* in Israel"). The latter might have been significant had the Greek used a messianic term for "ruler" but *archon* is in fact a very common word. It is thus the final phrase that lends *gravitas* to the promise, though its precise meaning is difficult to determine. Clearly something belongs to the distant past ("from of old, from ancient days") and the NRSV's use of the singular ("origin") could suggest pre-existence. However, the Hebrew word is plural (NIV/NJB: "origins"), which was rendered by the plural of *exodos* in the Greek (hence "departures" or "goings forth"). This suggests that it is his life, his "comings" and "goings," that are "from of old" and is probably therefore a reference to ancient prophecies. Further, since the context concerns "Bethlehem," the ancient prophecies are probably those concerning a future Davidic king. This appears to be confirmed by what follows: he will shepherd his people and his fame will spread to the ends of the earth (Mic 5:4).[4]

It is therefore surprising that Mic 5:2 is never quoted in the Dead Sea Scrolls or in any of the texts discussed in the last chapter. Given the variety of expectations and the large number of texts quoted in the scrolls, one would have expected at least some mention of this text or an interest in something special happening in Bethlehem. This inevitably puts a question mark against the authenticity of Matt 2:5–6 and John 7:42, which assume it was common knowledge that the Messiah would be born in

---

4. Themes that occur in Davidic texts like Ezek 34:23 ("I will set up over them one shepherd, my servant David, and he shall feed them: he shall feed them and be their shepherd") and Ps 2:8 ("Ask of me, and I will make the nations your heritage, and the ends of the earth your possession").

Bethlehem. A possible explanation is that once a place has become notorious (e.g., Pearl Harbor, Hiroshima), it is very difficult to imagine that it was once just an "ordinary" town or city before that event. We know from the second century that Bethlehem held great significance for the church and so perhaps Matthew and John assumed that this was also the case in Jesus' day. Some will find this explanation unduly skeptical but it actually offers a strong argument that Jesus was born in Bethlehem, as C. H. Dodd noted:

> [F]ar from the nativity stories in Matthew and Luke having been composed for apologetic purposes, in order to meet a generally held belief that the Messiah must be born in Bethlehem, it was the fact that Jesus was actually born there that revived in Christian circles interest in a prophecy which played little part in contemporary Jewish thought.[5]

If this is the case, then Matthew and Luke are both trying to draw out the significance of Jesus' birth in Bethlehem for their readers. Matthew, in keeping with his quotation style, goes to Scripture to find a suitable text and not surprisingly finds Mic 5:2, the only text to mention Bethlehem in the context of a future promise. The irony that the text speaks about the *insignificance* of Bethlehem is not lost on him and he inserts, in a rather obvious way, the Greek word *oudamos* ("by no means") to reverse the meaning. Indeed, it seems to him that the text is so clear and transparent that he cannot imagine anyone with an interest in Scripture not seeing its significance, and so he "creates" a dialogue where the priests and scribes quote the text in answer to Herod's question. Luke, on the other hand, remembers that there was a census around the time of Jesus' birth and draws on the broader scriptural theme that God controls the events of human history. For him, it is providential that such a decree should have taken Joseph and Mary from their home in Nazareth to Bethlehem, though he does not link this directly with Mic 5:2. For Luke, it is enough that God is orchestrating the events that will lead to the proclamation of the gospel throughout the known world (Acts 1:8).

If this scenario is broadly correct, then Jesus was born in Bethlehem and a case can be made that this is a fulfillment of Mic 5:2. The actual story has been embroidered, just as the quotation has been modified, but only to draw out the significance of the event for his readers. In particular, the role of Herod and the priests/scribes mirror what will happen at the end of Jesus' life. Herod, like Pilate, is unaware of the scriptural promises and so

---

5. Dodd, *Interpretation of the Fourth Gospel*, 91.

becomes an unwitting—though culpable—agent in the events that unfold. The priests/scribes do know the scriptural promises but refuse to join the magi in paying homage to Jesus, just as the priests/scribes in Jerusalem will refuse to follow the disciples in their commitment to Jesus.

Those who wish to uphold the authenticity of Matt 2:5–6/John 7:42 and argue that the Bethlehem promise was well known in Jesus' day point to two texts from the Aramaic translations of Scripture known as targums. These are notoriously difficult to date and could be as late as the fourth century C.E. However, it can be argued that Jewish tradition was hardly likely to "invent" promises about Bethlehem once it had become a place of pilgrimage for Christians, and so even if the date of composition is late, the Bethlehem tradition that it records might well be early. The Aramaic texts are on Mic 5:2 itself and Gen 35:20–21, where Bethlehem is mentioned in connection with the death of Rachel.

> And you, O Bethlehem Ephrathah, you who were too small to be numbered among the thousands of the house of Judah, from you shall come forth before me the anointed One (*meshiha*), to exercise dominion over Israel, he whose *name* was mentioned from of old, from ancient times. (*Tg. Mic.* 5:2)

> And Rachel died, and was buried in the way to Ephrath, which is Bethlehem. And Jakob erected a pillar over the house of burying: which is the pillar of the tomb of Rachel unto this day. And Jakob proceeded and spread his tent beyond the tower of Eder, *the place from whence, it is to be, the King Meshiha will be revealed at the end of the days.* (*Tg. Ps.-J.* Gen 35:20–21)

The targum of Mic 5:2 largely follows the Hebrew text but specifically says that it is the *Meshiha* ("Messiah" in English), that will come forth from Bethlehem. It also says that it is his *name* that is from of old, perhaps a deliberate attempt to exclude the Christian idea of Jesus' pre-existence. This tradition has then been used to interpret Gen 35:20–21, where the words in italics are not found in the Hebrew text but are an interpretative expansion. Two things are worthy of note. First, it is now *King Meshiha* who comes from Bethlehem, thus forging a link with the scriptural promises of a future Davidic king. Second, the Messiah will be revealed at the end of days, a tradition we have already observed in the Qumran scrolls (4Q174, 4Q161) and *4 Ezra* 12:32.

If these two texts, along with Matt 2:5–6 and John 7:42, are taken as evidence that it was common knowledge that the Messiah would come from Bethlehem, then we have to ask whether Matthew and Luke might have constructed or at least embroidered their stories in order to fit the prophecies. Before we can answer this, we first need to consider Matthew's guiding star and Luke's fortuitous census.

THE STAR AND THE CENSUS

The question of whether there really was a star that led the magi to Bethlehem has been a source of debate all through the centuries. Some have sought to correlate it with a particular conjunction of planets, the appearance of a comet or a supernova or new star.[6] However, the problem with all of these explanations is that it is difficult to see how such a phenomenon could have pointed out a particular house. It is perhaps possible to imagine how a sudden brightness in the sky could be interpreted as "go West" (the magi are said to be from the East) but hardly the specific path to Jerusalem, followed by a five or six mile journey down south to Bethlehem. This is not a modern objection; in a homily on Matt 6:6, Chrysostom (347–407 C.E.), Archbishop of Constantinople, said that "by reasons of its immense height, it could not sufficiently distinguish so confined a spot, and discover it to them that were desiring it."[7] Others have therefore suggested a supernatural phenomenon, rather like the story of the Israelites being guided through the wilderness by a "pillar of fire" (Exod 13:21). An obvious objection is that a pillar of fire is not a star, but perhaps that is being too literal. Matthew wants his readers to believe that God led the magi to Bethlehem by a "guiding star," a supernatural event that led them to the very house where Jesus was born. It was not a "natural" event that is open to scientific confirmation. As Luz notes, it is somewhat ironic that those who seek to defend the historicity of the star by pointing to a particular brightness at about that time do so at the expense of the miraculous nature of the story.[8]

6. The swift movement across the sky of a comet comes closest to what Matthew describes, but the seventy-seven year orbit of Halley's comet would have been too early (c. 12–11 B.C.E.) and we know of no other comet that fits the bill. A conjunction of Mars, Jupiter, and Saturn is bright enough to be visible in daylight and there is some evidence that this occurred in 7–6 B.C.E. Closest in time appears to be a nova or supernova around 5–4 B.C.E. and observed by Chinese astronomers (See Brown, *Birth of Jesus*, 170–73; Keener, *Matthew*, 102).

7. Quoted in Davies and Allison, *Matthew*, 247.

8. "Those who want to rescue the historicity of the story by minimizing its miracles destroy its message" (Luz, *Matthew 1–7*, 106 n. 42).

This does, however, raise the possibility of an altogether different explanation. The promise that "a star shall come out of Jacob, and a scepter shall rise out of Israel" (Num 24:17) was understood as messianic in the Qumran scrolls (CD 7:18–20) and in the targums, where "star" is replaced by "king" and "scepter" is replaced either by "Messiah" (*Tg. Onq.*; *Tg. Ps.-J.*) or "savior" (*Tg. Neof.*).[9] Could it be that Matthew was fully aware that stars do not hover over houses but was offering a fulfillment of Scripture in narrative form? Numbers 24:17 occurs in the Balaam narratives (Num 22–24) and Brown observes a number of other parallels: Balaam came from the East (23:7[10]); he came with two servants (22:22), making three in total; he is called a *magos* by Philo (*Moses* 1:276); he foiled the plan of King Balak to destroy Israel; and when his work was finished, he "got up and went back to his place" (24:25), just as the magi "left for their own country" (Matt 2:12). There are, of course, differences between the stories, notably that Balaam predicts the rising of a star, referring to a future ruler, whereas the magi *follow* a star, which directs them *to* the Messiah. Nevertheless, many commentators accept this interpretation and see it as part of Matthew's strategy to indicate the future inclusion of the Gentiles:

> The echoes of the Balaam story would remind the reader familiar with the Bible and Jewish midrashic tradition that already in the OT God had revealed His salvific intent to Gentiles. The presence of Gentile worshipers in Matthew's community was not the result of a failure in God's plan for Israel; it was the continuity and fulfillment of a plan of salvation for those from afar to be accomplished through the Messiah and Israel.[11]

9. A messianic interpretation is already detectable in the LXX, where "a scepter will arise from Israel" has become "a man shall rise up out of Israel."

10. The Greek verb *anatello* means "rising" but since the sun rises in the East, it is also used for direction. Most scholars find it significant that Matthew uses the cognate noun *anatole* in 2:2 and 2:9, which means "in the East" (RSV, NIV) but is probably also an allusion to Num 24:17 ("at its rising"—NRSV).

11. Brown, *Birth of the Messiah*, 196. Davies and Allison (*Matthew*, 234–35) note that early Christians such as Justin, Irenaeus, Origen, and Eusebius saw Num 24:17 as key to understanding Matthew's star. Gundry (*Matthew*, 27) says: "The star they have seen at its rising corresponds to and derives from the royal star seen to rise by Balaam." France (*Gospel of Matthew*, 62) calls it a "likely influence" but Blomberg ("Matthew," 5) remains cautious ("the magi *may* replace Balaam as unlikely Gentile witnesses to God's redemption"). However, Nolland (*Matthew*, 111) thinks it is unlikely, arguing that the differences far outweigh the similarities. Crossan and Borg (*First Christmas*, 144) agree with the Balaam allusion but also suggest that it is "Matthew's most obvious allusion to Roman imperial theology and the birth story of the Julian tribal family from Venus and

It has also been suggested that the gifts brought by the magi have a scriptural background. Thus the "rising star" of the Balaam narrative easily connects with the "rising light" of Isa 60:1, a passage which goes on to speak about the inclusion of Gentiles and the giving of gifts ("Nations shall come to your light . . . the wealth of the nations shall come to you. . . . They shall bring gold and frankincense"—60:3a, 5b, 6b). Further, Matthew speaks of paying homage (*proskuneo*) three times in this passage (Matt 2:2, 8, 11), which could suggest that he had a particular text in mind. The best candidate is Ps 72:10–11, which connects "kings," "gifts," and "homage" ("may the kings of Sheba and Seba bring gifts . . . all kings fall down [*proskuneo*] before him").[12]

Of course, discovering a scriptural background for the star, magi, and gifts does not necessarily mean that the events did not happen, but if their historicity is doubted on other grounds, then it offers additional support. We have already seen that there are good reasons for doubting an actual star leading the magi to a particular house. Brown suggests that there are also good reasons for doubting the visit of the magi, for if such an entourage had actually visited a particular house in a small town like Bethlehem, it is incredible that Herod could not ascertain which house had been visited in order to eliminate Jesus. It is true that Herod is known to have been a cruel leader and so ordering the killing of "all the children in and around Bethlehem who were two years old or under" (Matt 2:16) would not be out of character,[13] but there is no evidence that such a slaughter ever took place. It is not mentioned in Luke, Josephus, or any other historical source.[14]

Some have countered this by saying that a small town like Bethlehem probably had a population of only about 1,000 and given the high mortality

---

Anchises through Aeneas to Julus and thereafter." They also note that it was the star of Venus that led the Trojan refugees westward to Italy.

12. So Brown (*Birth of the Messiah*, 187–88); Gundry (*Matthew*, 32), who adds Song 3:6; 4:6 to account for the myrrh, and Davies and Allison (*Matthew*, 248–51), who think that Matthew is also drawing parallels between Jesus and Solomon: the gifts have strong temple connections; Solomon was thought to be the author of Ps 72; and the Queen of Sheba brings him gifts. On the other hand, Powell (*Chasing*, 138) notes that if the allusion was as clear as this, it is surprising that it took until the Middle Ages before the magi were regarded as kings.

13. Although not denying the importance of the fulfillment of Scripture, Richard Horsley argues that Matthew is deliberately highlighting the role of Herod as the agent of imperial domination, just as Luke's mention of the census would remind readers of the tribute that subjugated peoples must pay. See Horsley, *The Liberation of Christmas*.

14. Brown, *Birth of the Messiah*, 205–6.

rates, the actual number of children under two would not have been large. This is further reduced if "two years old or under" really means "just two or under" and so we could be talking about no more than twenty children. On the other hand, the citation of Jer 31:15 in Matt 2:18 ("A voice was heard in Ramah, wailing and loud lamentation, Rachel weeping for her children; she refused to be consoled, because they are no more") likens the grief in Bethlehem to the time of the exile, which affected the whole nation. There is also the obvious parallel with Pharaoh's "slaughter of the innocents," which led to the exodus. Thus the attempt to minimize the numbers involved in order to bolster the case for historicity runs counter to the effect the story is aiming to produce: this was a calamity on the scale of previous suffering of God's people, first in Egypt and then in Babylon. Although certainty is impossible, it does seem that Brown is correct that many of the details of the star, magi, and gifts have been "constructed" from Scripture.[15]

What about Luke's census? Josephus supports the statement that there was a census when Quirinius was governor (legate) of Syria for the purposes of taxation (*Ant.* 18:1–4). He also notes that a certain Judas led a rebellion against it, as is also mentioned by Luke in Acts 5:37 ("After him Judas the Galilean rose up at the time of the census and got people to follow him; he also perished, and all who followed him were scattered"). However, Quirinius did not occupy this position until 6 C.E., which would require Jesus to be born some ten years after the death of Herod in 4 B.C.E. This directly contradicts Matthew's statement that Jesus' birth was in "the time of King Herod" (Matt 2:1) and indeed Luke's own statement that the conception of John the Baptist was in "the days of King Herod" (Luke 1:5). There are three main ways that this has been explained. The first was put forward by Tertullian in the second century, who suggested that the original text of Luke 2:2 must have read Saturninus, who governed Syria between 6–4 B.C.E. Later scribes then changed this to Quirinius because his census was well known, whereas a census under Saturninus was otherwise unknown. However, there is no textual evidence to support this and the point that the census under Saturninus was unknown is itself evidence that there was in fact no census at that time.

The second suggestion is that Quirinius had an earlier governorship of Syria, perhaps between Saturninus and Varus, though this contradicts what

15. France (*Gospel of Matthew*, 83) defends the historicity of the event, stating that "on the scale of atrocities known to have been perpetrated by Herod during his later years this would register very low." However, later tradition moved in the opposite direction, exaggerating the numbers involved (14,000 in the Byzantine liturgy).

Josephus says ("Now Quintilius Varus was at this time at Jerusalem, being sent to succeed Saturninus as governor of Syria"—*Ant.* 17:89). A variation of this is that Quirinius acted as co-governor for a time but this would be unusual and again, there is no evidence to support it. The third solution is that the Greek word *protos* in Luke 2:2, usually translated "first" ("This was the *first* registration") could be translated as "earlier" or "before" and then taken with the Quirinius clause. This is favored by Nolland, who translates the verse: "This registration happened *before* Quirinius was governor of Syria."[16]

The problem with all of these solutions is that if there was a census in Herod's time, it must have been a small local affair as it is not mentioned in any of our sources. This is not in itself a problem, but it hardly fits with Luke's grand opening: "In those days a decree went out from Emperor Augustus that all the world should be registered" (Luke 2:1). One can just about imagine a census of Judea that required Jews to return to the place of their fathers, but on a world scale it would be strategically impossible. And since the purpose of a census was taxation, it is hard to see why it would be necessary, for the focus would be on where people lived and worked not their ancestral origins. It would seem that Luke inherited the tradition that Jesus was born in Bethlehem and knew of a census around that time and put the two together. He is clearly making the general point that God is in control of history, but there is debate as to the specific point that he intending to make.

A common interpretation is that Luke is wishing to contrast the *political* power wielded by Augustus (and Herod, his Client-King) with the *spiritual* power that will characterize Jesus' kingship. As Brown says, "The birthday worthy of divine honor and marking the true new beginning of time took place not in Rome but in Bethlehem."[17] Horsley, however, thinks that this is the result of importing later Christian understandings into the text. There is nothing in the infancy narratives, he says, to suggest that traditional Jewish hopes for liberation were fundamentally mistaken. The promises in the infancy canticles ("brought down the powerful from their thrones"; "rescued from the hands of our enemies"—Luke 1:52; 74) shows that the context of the juxtaposition of the census and the birth of Jesus is "the height of political-economic-religious conflict: the messiah now being

---

16. Nolland, *Luke 1—9:20*, 96. A fourth solution is that Josephus was mistaken and that Quirinius was governor during Herod's reign, though there is no mention of this in Tacitus, who also has an account of the period.

17. Brown, *Birth of the Messiah*, 416.

born would lead the people's successful resistance against that false and intolerable lordship and subjection."[18]

NAZARETH

That Jesus grew up in Nazareth is not in doubt; the problem is how Matthew can claim that this is a fulfillment of the words, "He will be called a Nazorean," when such a text cannot be found in any extant biblical manuscript. There are two main issues here. The first is whether calling Jesus a "Nazorean" (Greek: *Nazoraios*) is supposed to evoke something other than the fact that he grew up in Nazareth. The two main suggestions are that the word would evoke either the *nazir* ("Nazirite") of texts like Num 6:2, Judg 13:5, 7, and 1 Sam 1:11, or the *neser* ("branch") of Isa 11:1. The second issue is how Matthew thought the words, "He will be called a Nazorean," constitute an actual quotation of Scripture. Does he have a particular text in mind or is he combining a number of texts, as he did with Mic 5:2 and 2 Sam 5:2?

The linguistic evidence points more in the direction of *nazir* ("Nazirite"), for this is generally rendered in the LXX by the Greek word *naziraios*, which only differs from *Nazoraios* by a single letter. When it is not transliterated as *naziraios*, it is translated as "holy,"[19] and since Jesus was known as "the holy one" (Mark 1:24; Luke 4:34; John 6:69), it is easy to see how this would have appealed to Matthew. Jesus grew up in Nazareth, a town whose name evokes holiness and dedication to God. In addition, the context of the *nazir* texts in Judg 13 and 1 Sam 1 is the promise of a miraculous birth and the wording of Judg 13:7 (*"Behold, you shall conceive and bear a son . . . the boy shall be a Nazirite to God"*—RSV) is close to Isa 7:14 (*"Behold, a young woman shall conceive and bear a son, and shall call his name Immanuel"*—RSV), a text quoted in Matt 1:23.[20]

On the other hand, one of the main characteristics of a Nazirite is asceticism (Num 6:2; Judg 13:4–5; 1 Sam 1:11), something that Jesus affirms of John the Baptist but denies for himself: "For John came neither eating

18. Horsley, *Liberation of Christmas*, 38. He also suggests that the visit of the magi is not so much a symbol for the inclusion of the Gentiles but "the longing among eastern peoples generally, not just the Jews, for a restoration of their own native rule against the alien western imperial rule" (ibid., 58).

19. Judg 13:5 in Codex Alexandrinus (A) and Judg 13:7 in Codex Vaticanus (B).

20. Quotations from the RSV. The parallel is less obvious in the NRSV as it uses a more colloquial rendering for conception in Isa 7:14 ("the young woman is with child").

nor drinking, and they say, 'He has a demon'; the Son of Man came eating and drinking, and they say, 'Look, a glutton and a drunkard, a friend of tax collectors and sinners!'" (Matt 11:18–19). Granted, Jesus is using hyperbole (exaggeration) to make his point, it is nevertheless difficult to imagine Jesus identifying with the Nazirite vows. Indeed, Hagner suggests that the parallel between "holy" and "the holy one" is superficial, for Jesus had a very different understanding of holiness to the Nazirites.[21] Thus, while linguistically it is easy to imagine readers spotting a connection between "Nazareth" and "Nazirite," it is harder to see a connection in meaning.

This is why some scholars find the link with *neser* more convincing, even though it is linguistically more distant and the parallel only works in Hebrew, since the Greek for "branch" in Isa 11:1 is *anthos*. However, in terms of meaning, Isa 11:1 ("A shoot shall come out from the stump of Jesse, and a branch shall grow out of his roots") has much to commend it. It follows the promise of Emmanuel in Isa 7:14 and Matthew would have almost certainly assumed the two texts were talking about the same individual. Isaiah 11:1 was regarded as messianic at Qumran, as it is elsewhere in the New Testament (Heb 7:14; Rev 5:5). It is not difficult to see how Matthew might have regarded the insignificant village of "Nazareth" as appropriate for the messianic *neser*, though the link is far from obvious for Greek-speaking readers.[22]

What of our second question? How did Matthew think the specific words, "He shall be called a Nazorean," constitute a quotation? A clue would appear to lie in the introductory formula, as can be seen if we set it alongside the introductory formulae for the previous four quotations:

> All this took place to fulfill what had been spoken by the Lord *through the prophet* (1:22)
> for so it has been written *by the prophet* (2:5)
> This was to fulfill what had been spoken by the Lord *through the prophet* (2:15)
> Then was fulfilled what had been spoken *through the prophet Jeremiah* (2:17)

21. Hagner, *Matthew 1–13*, 41.

22. Brown (*Birth of the Messiah*, 223–25) and Davies and Allison (*Matthew*, 276–77) favor *nazir*, while Gundry (*Matthew*, 39–40) and Hagner (*Matthew 1–13*, 41) favor *neser*. Nolland (*Matthew*, 130) and Keener (*Matthew*, 114) are undecided but think the messianic *neser* is probably more likely. France (*Matthew*, 91–95) finds both solutions untenable and suggests that the quotation ("He will be called a Nazorean") means something like, "He shall be regarded as a non-entity." He then links this with passages of rejection/dejection like Zech 9–14, Isa 53, and Pss 22 and 69.

so that what had been spoken *through the prophets* might be fulfilled (2:23)

The plural "prophets" is unexpected and suggests that Matthew had more than one text in mind. If the primary allusion is to the *nazir*, then there are two main suggestions for the secondary text. The first is Isa 4:3 ("Whoever is left in Zion and remains in Jerusalem will be called holy"). Though the subject is plural, the passive verb ("will be called") is the same as Matthew's and we have already seen that there is a scriptural link between *nazir* and "holy." On this view, Matthew's quotation is a combination of Isa 4:3 ("will be called") and Judg 13:5 or 7 (*naziraios*). The second suggestion, argued particularly by Maarten Menken,[23] is that the secondary text is Isa 7:14, where the verb for "calling" is in the singular. If this is correct, then Matthew begins and ends the infancy narrative with a quotation of Isa 7:14 ("Behold, a young woman shall conceive and bear a son, and *shall call* his name Immanuel"—RSV), to which he make's two additions: the child will also be called Jesus, because "he will save his people from their sins" (Matt 1:21), and Nazorean, because he comes from Nazareth (2:23).

If the primary allusion is to the *neser* of Isa 11:1, then the link with Isa 7:14 is even more obvious as the chapters closely follow one another. There is also a possible connection with Isa 4:2 ("On that day the branch of the LORD shall be beautiful and glorious, and the fruit of the land shall be the pride and glory of the survivors of Israel"). It is true that this uses a different word for "branch" (*semah*) but the two words are virtually synonyms in the Hebrew Bible and the connection opens up the possibility of evoking other important "branch" texts, like Jer 23:5 and Zech 3:8.

Certainty is clearly impossible, but one thing we can be definite about is the movement of thought. No one seriously believes that Matthew's meditation on Scripture, whether focused on the *nazir* texts or the *neser* of Isa 11:1, led to the "creation" of Nazareth as Jesus' hometown. As we noted at the beginning of the chapter, "Jesus of Nazareth" is firmly lodged in the tradition before Matthew. It would appear that Matthew saw the potential of the name Nazareth to evoke important themes from Scripture, even if the precise nature of those themes is unclear to us. Does this tip the balance in favor of the view that Jesus really was born in Bethlehem? I am inclined to think it does. Luke's census looks like a deliberate attempt to get Jesus to Bethlehem but not so that his birth fulfilled the promise of Mic 5:2, which is never mentioned. It seems more likely that he knew of a tradition that

23. Menken, *Matthew's Bible*, 161–77.

Jesus was born in Bethlehem and coupled it with the tradition of a census that happened around that time (Luke was writing some eighty years later), in order to make an anti-imperialist point.

Matthew also inherited the tradition that Jesus was born in Bethlehem but his style was to go to Scripture to illuminate its meaning. Although he gives the impression that a messianic interpretation of Mic 5:2 was well known at the time, its non-appearance in the Dead Sea Scrolls or other contemporary documents suggests otherwise. It does occur in two late targums and some have argued that this probably represents early tradition, since Jews would hardly have introduced it once it had become important for Christians. However, this is not as convincing as it sounds. For all we know, Jews of the fourth or fifth century might have focused on a messianic ruler from Bethlehem because it was evident to them that Jesus was not that figure. After all, Jerusalem had been destroyed and the people remain in subjection—this is not the messianic rule Scripture envisages.

CONCLUSION

This study of Bethlehem and Nazareth has led to two important conclusions. First, it is quite likely that Jesus was born in Bethlehem and brought up in Nazareth, as both Matthew and Luke affirm. The narratives that describe this contain a considerable amount of "poetic license" (a world-wide census and a moving star that can indicate a particular house) but it is very unlikely that the places themselves were generated from Scripture. The Bethlehem promise was not well known and the Nazareth promise, if it can be called that, is extremely obscure. The most likely conclusion is that Jesus really was born in Bethlehem and brought up in Nazareth.

However, before we can affirm that these elements of Jesus' birth were "according to Scripture," we have to consider the particular approach to Scripture found in each of the Gospels. Luke does not seek to link either place with a scriptural text but wishes to demonstrate that the birth of Jesus represents the "hope for a very different kind of world from the world of Pharaoh and Caesar, the world of domination and empire.[24] For those who accept that Jesus accomplished this, despite the current state of our world, then it might be possible to speak of "fulfillment," though not specifically of Bethlehem and Nazareth.

---

24. Crossan and Borg, *First Christmas*, 224.

However, Matthew's claim is more problematic because he cites a text that he has had to modify (Mic 5:2) and a text that does not exist. If the latter is an attempt to evoke the biblical *nazir* or *neser*, then it could be regarded as a fulfillment, though it would not be what most people today understand by the term. Indeed, one thing that is becoming clear in this study is that Matthew's quotations can only be regarded as fulfillments if they are understood in a particular way. For some, such a circular argument would instantly discredit his claim for fulfillment but others recognize an inevitable dialectic: Jesus illuminates the meaning of Scripture, while Scripture illuminates the meaning of Jesus. Such a dialectical understanding is not unique to the Bible: Harriet Davidson says of T. S. Eliot's *The Waste Land* that the "work alluded to reflects upon the present context even as the present context absorbs and changes the allusion."[25] In other words, we are never just dealing with two static entities, the original meaning of a text and its present contextual meaning, and then asking about the relationship between them. The very act of quotation juxtaposes texts and contexts, which mutually influence one another: "The work's meaning is in the tension between its previous contextual definition and its present context."[26]

One might therefore say that Matthew has drawn on the semantic potential of Mic 5:2 and one or more *nazir/neser* texts, given his belief that Jesus is the promised Messiah. It is clearly not identical to the original meaning but many literary theorists would say that this is inevitable. Meir Sternberg, for example, says: "However accurate the wording of the quotation and however pure the quoter's motives, tearing a piece of discourse from its original habitat and recontextualizing it within a new network of relations cannot but interfere with its effect."[27] On this understanding, it might be possible to speak of Bethlehem and Nazareth as "fulfillments" in that they can be plotted on a plausible trajectory of meaning. The question then becomes: is the destination of the trajectory regarded as correct? Crossan and Borg put it like this:

> In our judgment, there was no special star, no wise men, and no plot by Herod to kill Jesus. So is the story factually true? No. But as parable, is it true? For us as Christians, the answer is a robust affirmative. Is Jesus light shining in the darkness? Yes. Do the Herods of this world seek to extinguish the light? Yes. Does Jesus still shine in the darkness? Yes.[28]

25. Davidson, *T. S. Eliot and Hermeneutics*, 117.
26. Ibid.
27. Sternberg, "Proteus in Quotation-Land," 108.
28. Crossan and Borg, *First Christmas*, 184.

4

Egypt and Ramah

INTRODUCTION

In between the quotations concerning Jesus' birth in Bethlehem (Matt 2:6) and growing up in Nazareth (Matt 2:23), there are two further quotations which also mention particular places. The first is from Hos 11:1, a text which refers back to the exodus, where God called his people (Hebrew: "my son") out of Egypt. The second is from Jer 31:15, a text which refers to the "lamentation and bitter weeping" in Ramah, as God's people are taken off into exile (Jer 40:1). It is clearly of great importance to Matthew that these key events in Israel's history are being repeated in the events surrounding Jesus' birth and he even speaks of their *fulfillment*:

> Now after they had left, an angel of the Lord appeared to Joseph in a dream and said, "Get up, take the child and his mother, and flee to Egypt, and remain there until I tell you; for Herod is about to search for the child, to destroy him." Then Joseph got up, took the child and his mother by night, and went to Egypt, and remained there until the death of Herod. This was to fulfill what had been spoken by the Lord through the prophet, *"Out of Egypt I have called my son."* When Herod saw that he had been tricked by the wise men, he was infuriated, and he sent and killed all the children in and around Bethlehem who were two years old or under, according to the time that he had learned from the wise men. Then was fulfilled what had been spoken through the prophet Jeremiah: *"A voice was heard in Ramah, wailing and loud lamentation, Rachel*

weeping for her children; she refused to be consoled, because they are no more." (Matt 2:13–18)

We have already seen how certain events in the birth stories seem to mirror events or people in Scripture (promise of a miraculous birth; protection from a ruling power; foreigners traveling to pay homage). This is generally described as "typology," from the Greek word *typos*, meaning "pattern" or "example." Thus Paul can say that Israel's rebellions in the wilderness "occurred as examples (*typoi*) for us, so that we might not desire evil as they did" (1 Cor 10:6). More significantly, in Rom 5:12–21, Paul uses the story of Adam's disobedience and its destructive consequences to highlight what Christ has accomplished: "Therefore just as one man's trespass led to condemnation for all, so one man's act of righteousness leads to justification and life for all" (Rom 5:18). Though Christ is not like Adam in character, they do have one thing in common: their actions have consequences for all of humanity, and so Paul can call Adam a "type (*typos*) of the one who was to come" (Rom 5:14).

However, neither of these examples uses the word "fulfill" to explain the connection. A closer parallel to Matthew is John 3:14, where Jesus is recorded as saying: "And just as Moses lifted up the serpent in the wilderness, *so must* the Son of Man be lifted up, that whoever believes in him may have eternal life." The reference is to the story in Num 21:8–9, where the Israelites were healed of their snake bites when they gazed upon a bronze serpent that Moses had placed on a pole. The parallel is presumably that people can be healed of their sins if they gaze upon Jesus (as Son of Man) when he is placed on a (type of) pole, namely, the cross. John does not use the word "fulfill" but he does speak of the necessity (*dei*) of Jesus being lifted up so that people might believe.[1]

Thus the key question in this chapter is the validity or otherwise of "typological fulfillment." The parallels between God calling Israel ("my son") out of Egypt and "Rachel . . . weeping for her children . . . because they are no more" (Jer 31:15) at the exile are no doubt instructive but in what sense have they been "fulfilled" in the events surrounding Jesus' birth? Before we attempt to answer this, we must first clarify how each quotation

---

1. One might think that John was drawn to the words of Num 21:8–9 because Moses "lifted up the serpent" but the Numbers text does not specifically say this. It is of course a reasonable deduction, for a crowd of people could not gaze at the bronze serpent unless it was "lifted up," but it might be that the events surrounding the death of Jesus (or perhaps even the ascension) have influenced John's reading of the Numbers story.

is being used and how this relates both to its original context and how it was understood in the first century.[2]

HOSEA 11:1

The context of Hos 11:1 is an explanation for why Israel is about to be destroyed by the Assyrians. The preceding verse says: "Thus it shall be done to you, O Bethel, because of your great wickedness. At dawn the king of Israel shall be utterly cut off" (10:15). Israel is accused of corruption (9:9), wickedness (9:15), idolatry (10:1), insincere devotion (10:4), and injustice (10:13). As a result, they shall "return to the land of Egypt, and Assyria shall be their king, because they have refused to return to me" (11:5). The irony of the punishment is, of course, that God had previously rescued them from Egypt and brought them into the promised land. Now they are to return to Egypt and slavery again. Indeed, the context of Hos 11:1 is that such wicked behavior has characterized Israel from the moment they left Egypt:

> When Israel was a child, I loved him, and *out of Egypt I called my son.* The more I called them, the more they went from me; they kept sacrificing to the Baals, and offering incense to idols. (Hos 11:1–2)

Since Matthew hardly wants to compare Jesus with the idolatry of Israel, he is presumably intending a contrast: Jesus accomplishes that which Israel failed to accomplish. Matthew is helped in this by the fact that the Hebrew text of Hos 11:1 refers to Israel as "my son" and of course he firmly believes that Jesus is God's Son (3:17; 4:3, 6; 8:29; 14:33; 16:16; 26:63; 27:40).[3] Thus according to France, Matthew's succinct quotation

---

2. It should be noted that not all scholars accept that we are dealing with typology here. In a famous debate conducted in the *Westminster Theological Journal* (Vol. 63, 2001), John Sailhamer argued that if Hos 11:1 is read in context, it should be seen as predictive prophecy—God will bring his Messiah out of Egypt just as he formerly brought Israel out of Egypt. To support this, he claimed that Hosea was not simply referring to the exodus event but to its interpretation in the rest of the Pentateuch. In particular, Balaam's prophecy in Num 24 contains the phrase, "God who brings *him* out of Egypt" (24:8), which Hosea would have understood as a reference to the Messiah. Few have found this convincing and it was challenged by Dan McCartney and Peter Enns in the same volume.

3. The LXX appears to have taken "Israel" as the name of the patriarch Jacob (Gen 32:28) and so continues "and out of Egypt I called his children." This is corrected in the versions of Theodotion, Aquila, and Symmachus, and Menken (*Matthew's Bible*, 133–42) suggests that Matthew is probably using a text that had also been corrected, though many scholars think that Matthew is simply offering his own translation of the Hebrew.

expresses in the most economical form a wide-ranging theology of the new exodus and of Jesus as the true Israel which will play a significant role throughout Matthew's gospel. As usual, Matthew's christological interpretation consists not of exegesis of what the text quoted meant in its original context, but of a far-reaching theological argument which takes the OT text and locates it within an over-arching scheme of fulfillment which finds in Jesus the end point of numerous prophetic trajectories. When Jesus "came out of Egypt," that was to be the signal for a new exodus in which Jesus would fill the role not only of the God-sent deliverer but also of God's "son" Israel himself.[4]

If this is the case, then we have to ask whether Matthew's desire to present such a theology has led him to invent a "flight to Egypt," so that Jesus can subsequently leave it. It is not mentioned in Luke and it is difficult to see where it could fit, for Luke says that once Mary, Joseph, and Jesus "had finished everything required by the law of the Lord, they returned to Galilee, to their own town of Nazareth" (2:39). The quotation in Luke 2:24 ("a pair of turtledoves or two young pigeons") shows that this refers to the laws of purification after childbirth (Lev 12:1–8), which stipulate that a male child must be circumcised on the eighth day and that the mother will be in a state of impurity for forty days, after which a sacrifice is to be offered. Luke confusingly speaks of *their* purification and connects it with the archaic law to redeem the first-born son (Exod 13:13).[5] Despite this confusion, it is clear that Luke envisages Jesus and his family returning to Nazareth shortly after the stipulated forty day were completed. If Matthew and Luke are to be harmonized, we would have to posit a return to Bethlehem some time later and then a flight to Egypt. This is not in itself impossible but a return to their home in Nazareth is hardly a natural reading of Matt 2:21–23, where Joseph is warned in a dream not to return to Judea and so traveled to Galilee and "made his home in a town called Nazareth."

Commentators have also pointed out that the position of the quotation in Matthew is awkward, as one would have expected a quotation that supports the preceding statement that Jesus and his family "remained" in Egypt. This is precisely what Gundry argues when he says that Matthew

4. France, *Matthew*, 81.

5. Archaic because Num 3:12 states that the Levites now perform that function: "I hereby accept the Levites from among the Israelites as substitutes for all the firstborn that open the womb among the Israelites." Some manuscripts read "his purification" and one manuscript reads "her purification," almost certainly later attempts to remove the difficulty.

"is not highlighting Jesus' later departure from Egypt as a new Exodus, but God's preservation of Jesus in Egypt as a sign of his divine sonship: God cares for Jesus as a father cares for his son."[6] Theologically, this suggestion has much to commend it, for Egypt was a place of refuge for Joseph and his brothers during times of famine; it was only later when a "new king arose over Egypt, who did not know Joseph" (Exod 1:8) that it became a place of danger. However, it is difficult to see how the quotation, "out of Egypt I called my son," which clearly refers to the exodus, can be used to support this.[7] Most scholars think that Matthew is applying the quotation to Jesus' departure from Egypt but has particular reasons for placing it earlier in the narrative. The most common explanation is that the departure narrative (Matt 2:19–23) is intended to lead to the final quotation that Jesus "will be called a Nazarene." Had Matthew placed the quotation of Hos 11:1 after the statement that they left and traveled towards Judea (2:21), it would have clashed with the statement that they did not in fact go to Judea but were directed to Galilee, as can be seen if we make the transposition:

> Then Joseph got up, took the child and his mother, and went to the land of Israel. *This was to fulfill what had been spoken by the Lord through the prophet, "Out of Egypt I have called my son."* But when he heard that Archelaus was ruling over Judea in place of his father Herod, he was afraid to go there. And after being warned in a dream, he went away to the district of Galilee. There he made his home in a town called Nazareth, so that what had been spoken through the prophets might be fulfilled, "He will be called a Nazorean." (Matt 2:21, 15, 22–23)

Interestingly, this awkwardness has been used by some scholars to argue for the essential historicity of the "flight to Egypt." Thus Hos 11:1 is not a prophecy in its original context and is never quoted in the Dead Sea Scrolls or contemporary Jewish literature. There was therefore no necessity for Matthew to construct a fulfillment narrative, since no one thought it was a text that needed fulfilling. Indeed, since prophets like Isaiah (43:16–21), Jeremiah (16:14–15), and even Hosea himself (2:14–15) can use "exodus" language to describe a future deliverance, Matthew could have made his point even if Jesus was never in Egypt. Craig Evans concludes that the best

---

6. Gundry, *Matthew*, 34.

7. In his earlier work (*Use of the Old Testament in St. Matthew's Gospel*, 93–94), Gundry suggested that the Greek behind, "Out of Egypt I called my son," could also be rendered, "*Since* Egypt I called my son," but few have found this convincing and he does not mention it in his later commentary.

explanation for Matthew's rather unusual choice of Hos 11:1 and his some-what awkward placing of the quotation in the narrative is that there really was a "flight to Egypt" and so "we have here yet another example in which Matthew seeks out a passage from the prophets that he can apply, in a ty-pological sense, to an event in the life of Jesus."[8] It has also been noted that Egypt was outside the jurisdiction of Herod and contained a large Jewish population, so such a trip is historically quite plausible.

On the other hand, if the short quotation of Hos 11:1 is unlikely to have generated the "flight to Egypt" narrative, it is possible that the broader context of the quotation might have done so. Thus while Hos 11:1–7 con-tinues the theme of Israel rebellion and punishment, there is a dramatic change in verse 8, where God declares: "How can I give you up, Ephraim? How can I hand you over, O Israel? . . . My heart recoils within me . . ." In other words, Israel's punishment is not the final word, for there will be a new exodus where the people will "come trembling like birds from Egypt" and God will "return them to their homes" (11:11). This was partially fulfilled when Israel returned from exile, but Matthew sees its true fulfillment in the Christian community (Matt 19:28). Just as he will later speak of graves opening as a sign that the resurrection of the dead has begun (Matt 27:52; cf. Ezek 37:12), so he begins his story with Jesus and his family leaving Egypt as a sign that the new exodus has begun. It is not the case, therefore, that Matthew would have had no reason to invent a "flight to Egypt."

Alternatively, it is commonly recognized that Matthew is telling the story of Jesus in a way that mirrors the story of Moses. What is less known is that Moses' story had already been told and retold so that by the first century, it had gained a number of additional features. For example, in Josephus's account (*Ant.* 2.205–16), the reason that Pharaoh vowed to kill the Hebrew children was because a scribe had foretold the birth of a libera-tor, and this was communicated to Moses's father, Amram, in a dream:

> One of those sacred scribes, who are very sagacious in foretelling future events, truly told the king, that about this time there would be born a child to the Israelites, who, if he were reared, would bring the Egyptian dominion low, and would raise the Israelites; that he would excel all men in virtue, and obtain a glory that would be remembered through all ages. (*Ant.* 2.205)

8. Evans, *Matthew*, 65.

A man whose name was Amram, one of the nobler sort of the Hebrews, was afraid for his whole nation; . . . he betook himself to prayer to God, and entreated him to have compassion. . . . Accordingly God had mercy on him, and was moved by his supplication. He stood by him in his sleep, and exhorted him. . . . I shall provide for you all . . . this child of yours . . . shall deliver the Hebrew nation from the distress they are under from the Egyptians. His memory shall be famous while the universe lasts . . . (*Ant.* 2.210–16 abbreviated).

Charles Talbert concludes that for "anyone who knew the Moses legends in antiquity, it would have been impossible to miss the remarkable similarities between them and Matthew's story of Jesus' origins."[9] This can be seen in the following table:[10]

Moses	*Jesus*
A genealogy locates Moses within the line that runs from the patriarchs (Exod 1:1–5).	A genealogy locates Jesus within the line that runs from the patriarchs (Matt 1:2–16).
Amram heard in a dream that his son will save God's people (*Ant.* 2.210–15).	Joseph heard in a dream that his son will save God's people (Matt 1:21).
Pharaoh learned of the future deliverer from a sacred scribe (*Ant.* 2.205).	Herod learned of the future deliverer from the chief priests and scribes (Matt 2:4–6).
Pharaoh attempted to kill Moses by killing all the young male children (*Ant.* 2.205–9).	Herod attempted to kill Jesus by killing all the young male children (Matt 2:2–18).
Moses was forced to leave his homeland because Pharaoh wanted to kill him (Exod 2:15).	Jesus was forced to leave his homeland because Herod wanted to kill him (Matt 2:13–14).
After Pharaoh died, Moses was commanded by God to return to Egypt "for all the men who were seeking your life are dead" (Exod 4:19).	After Herod died, Joseph was commanded by God to return to Israel "for those who were seeking the child's life are dead" (Matt 2:20).

Thus it is possible that Matthew has constructed his narrative in order to show that Jesus is a "new Moses" leading a "new exodus" into a "new promised land." He will later have Jesus ascend a mountain (Luke 6:17 calls it a "plain") and deliver a "new teaching" (Matt 5:21, 27, 33, 38, 43), an obvious

9. Talbert, *Matthew*, 38.

10. Adapted from ibid., 38–39.

parallel to the giving of the Ten Commandments. On another occasion, Jesus will ascend a mountain and appear to his disciples with a face that "shone like the sun" (Matt 17:2), a parallel to Moses's experience in Exod 34:29 ("When Aaron and all the Israelites saw Moses, the skin of his face was shining, and they were afraid to come near him"). The only question then is why Matthew chose Hos 11:1 rather than a text from Exodus, but that is easily answered: he wanted a text from the prophets and "out of Egypt I called my son" is a succinct summary of the exodus narrative. Thus although Evans is probably correct that on its own, Hos 11:1 is unlikely to have generated the "flight to Egypt" narrative, it is possible that Matthew's desire to present a Jesus/Moses typology might have done so.[11]

It would appear then that there are plausible arguments on both sides and it is difficult to be sure whether Matthew moved from event to Scripture or Scripture to event. However, the issue is not crucial to the central question of this chapter, namely, the validity or otherwise typological fulfillment. In the troubled times of the first century, many people fled to Egypt and no doubt some of them returned when it was safe (or economically viable) to do so. That does not make them typological fulfillments of the Moses/exodus narrative and so the bare fact (if that is the case) that Jesus spent time in Egypt is not the issue. The question is whether the events of Jesus' birth can reasonably be said to "fulfill" or "complete" the exodus led by Moses?

Greg Beale says that in order to speak of typological fulfillment there must be more than an analogy or parallel between the two passages. He does not agree with scholars like Sailhamer and Kaiser,[12] who think that Hos 11:1 is a messianic prediction, but he does think that in order to qualify as typological fulfillment there must be something in the original context that points forward or foreshadows something in the future. In other words, it is not enough that the parallel or analogy is purely retrospective, even if the retrospective insight is thought of as inspired. To qualify as typological fulfillment, there must be some indication of a "foreshadowing"

---

11. Drawing on later Jewish sources, Roger Aus adds a number of other parallels (1) Moses' father Amram was regarded as righteous; (2) The Holy Spirit came upon Miriam (Moses' sister) and she prophesied that her mother Jochebed will bear a son who will save Israel; (3) When Amram heard that Pharaoh was going to kill the Hebrew children, he divorced his wife but was later persuaded to take her back; (4) Moses was weaned for two years, which might explain the instruction to kill the children "two years old or under" in Matt 2:16; (5) God giving children to barren women is sometimes referred to as a restoration of virginity. See Aus, *Matthew 1–2 and the Virginal Conception*.

12. Kaiser, *Use of the Old Testament in the New*, 47–53.

or "presignification" of future events.[13] His argument for Hos 11:1 has two aspects: (1) The broader context of Hos 11:1–11 shows that Hosea envisaged a future departure from Egypt patterned on the first exodus; and (2) The broader context of the whole book shows that Hosea envisaged this being accomplished by a future leader. We have already looked at the evidence for the first point but the second needs consideration. The two key texts are Hos 1:11 and 3:5:

> The people of Judah and the people of Israel shall be gathered together, and they shall appoint for themselves one head; and they shall take possession of the land, for great shall be the day of Jezreel. (1:11)

> Afterward the Israelites shall return and seek the LORD their God, and David their king; they shall come in awe [NIV: trembling] to the LORD and to his goodness in the latter days. (3:5)

Although it is not stated that the "head" in Hos 1:11 is the "king" of Hos 3:5, Beale thinks that there are enough "Egypt" connections to assume this. For example, he notes that there is a link between the people who come "trembling" to God in Hos 3:5 and those who come "trembling like birds from Egypt" in Hos 11:10–11. Admittedly, the link would have been stronger had they used the same Hebrew verb (hence NRSV "awe") but one can acknowledge the conceptual parallel. There is still quite a difference between the re-gathered tribes of Israel and the movement begun by Jesus as he leaves Egypt and so we are talking about "indirect" rather than "direct" fulfillment. But Beale thinks that there is a sufficient "foreshadowing" in Hosea to be able to speak of an "organic expansion or development of meaning," like that of "acorn to an oak tree, a bud to a flower, or a seed to an apple."[14]

> The pattern of the first exodus at the beginning of Israel's history will be repeated again at the end of Israel's history in the end time. It is unlikely that Hosea saw these two exoduses to be accidental or coincidental or unconnected similar events. Hosea appears to understand that Israel's first exodus (Hos. 11:1) was to be recapitulated at the time of the nation's latter-day exodus.[15]

---

13. Beale, *Handbook*, 14.

14. Ibid., 27.

15. Beale, *Biblical Theology*, 408.

JEREMIAH 31:15

Although there has been much debate about Matthew's use of Hos 11:1, his use of Jer 31:15 is even more puzzling. Matthew is telling the story of Jesus' birth as a parallel to the birth of Moses and so one would have expected a comparison between the grief caused by Herod's murderous actions and that caused by Pharaoh's.[16] Instead, we have a reference to Jer 31:15, where the pain of Judah's exile to Babylon is described in terms of Rachel, the wife of Jacob/Israel, weeping for her children "because they were no more." The weeping is located at a placed called Ramah, about six miles north of Jerusalem, which appears to have been a collection point before the exiles were transferred to Babylon (Jer 40:1). In the light of Isa 10:29 and Hos 5:8, Davies and Allison suggest that "Ramah might be regarded as a city of sadness *par excellence*,"[17] but unlike Bethlehem, Egypt, and Nazareth, it does not play a role in Matthew's narrative: Jesus never went to Ramah and the children were not slaughtered at Ramah. There are at least three difficulties concerning Matthew's claim that Herod's "slaughter of the innocents" is a fulfillment of Jer 31:15: (1) Jer 31:15 is not a prediction of a future event; (2) Given the suffering that lies ahead (Matt 24:21), it is hard to see how the deaths at Bethlehem "fill up" or "complete" the suffering of the exile; and (3) According to both the historical books (2 Kgs 24:3–4) and the prophets (Jer 1:15–16), Judah's exile is a punishment for sin and so is hardly a suitable parallel to the killing of Bethlehem's children.

The first is not a problem if we accept that we are dealing with "typology" rather than the fulfillment of a prediction. As with the quotation of Hos 11:1, the key question is whether the verb translated "fulfill" (*pleroo*) can reasonably be understood as "true in an escalated sense" or "brings to completion." A glance at both classical dictionaries and those that focus on the New Testament show that this is entirely possible, as can be seen from the following New Testament examples:

> And suddenly from heaven there came a sound like the rush of a violent wind, and it filled (*pleroo*) the entire house where they were sitting. (Acts 2:2)

16. Aus notes that in the Jewish midrashim (Zohar, Shemoth), Rabbi Judah connects Jochebed's weeping with Jer 31:15 and concludes that it is "most probable that the Evangelist Matthew already found Jer 31:15 in the Palestinian Jewish Christian haggadic development of the Jesus birth narrative available to him. He then added his own emphasis on the Scripture's now being 'fulfilled'" (*Matthew 1–2*, 29).

17. Davies and Allison, *Matthew*, I.269.

> After Jesus had finished (*pleroo*) all his sayings in the hearing of the people, he entered Capernaum. (Luke 7:1)

> I became its servant according to God's commission that was given to me for you, to make the word of God fully known (*pleroo*). (Col 1:25)

> Then after completing (*pleroo*) their mission Barnabas and Saul returned to Jerusalem and brought with them John, whose other name was Mark. (Acts 12:25)

In Acts 2:1, the verb is used to express the extent of the sound: it *filled* the entire house. It does not look back to any previous event and so there is no sense of "fulfillment"; it is simply used for emphasis.[18] In Luke 7:1, the verb is usually translated "finished" (NRSV, NIV) or "ended" (KJV, RSV). Col 1:25 is more explicit: the word of God was made known *because* God had commissioned it. There is a correspondence between a previous event (the commission) and the present action (making God's word known). The KJV actually uses the word "fulfill" here ("Whereof I am made a minister, according to the dispensation of God which is given to me for you, to fulfill the word of God"). However, the NIV moves in a different direction ("to present to you the word of God *in its fullness*"). The sense of "completion" is uppermost in Acts 12:25 and this time the RSV follows the KJV in using the word "fulfilled." The verse looks back to Acts 11:29, where Barnabas and Saul are sent by the church in Antioch to take a relief fund to Jerusalem and they return when their task has been completed/fulfilled.[19]

In view of this diversity, there is no reason to insist that Matthew must have direct fulfillment in mind when he uses *pleroo*: he could be using the verb more generally to mean, "true in an escalated sense," or "true in the sense of completion." This then brings us to the second point: in what sense can Herod's slaughter be considered as an "escalation" or "completion" of the pain suffered by the exiles? It is clearly not an escalation in a quantitative sense, as it only affects one village and only one age group within that village. The suffering experienced at the exile is far greater than that

18. It is quite probable that Luke understands the Pentecost event as looking back to various scriptural texts, but this verse is simply concerned with the sound of the phenomenon.

19. There is a textual problem with this verse as important Greek manuscripts read "to Jerusalem," which suggests the mission is not the relief fund in Acts 11:30 but the work in Antioch in Acts 11:26.

experienced in Bethlehem. Neither can it be said to "complete" the suffering of God's people, as Matt 24:21 predicts far greater sufferings in the future ("For at that time there will be great suffering, such as has not been from the beginning of the world until now, no, and never will be"). One could perhaps speak of "escalation" in that the suffering now extends to the innocent, whereas 2 Chr 36:15–21 views the exile as a punishment for sin.[20] However, it has to be said that Matthew does not emphasize the innocence of the Bethlehem children, and in any case, the infants who suffered during the exile were surely as innocent as those in Bethlehem.

As a result, most scholars suggest that the parallel that Matthew has in mind is not "suffering" as such but the combination of suffering followed by deliverance. The context of Jer 31:15 is that Rachel should weep no more because salvation is about to follow:

> Thus says the LORD: A voice is heard in Ramah, lamentation and bitter weeping. Rachel is weeping for her children; she refuses to be comforted for her children, because they are no more. Thus says the LORD: Keep your voice from weeping, and your eyes from tears; for there is a reward for your work, says the LORD: they shall come back from the land of the enemy; there is hope for your future, says the LORD: your children shall come back to their own country. (Jer 31:15–17)

Indeed, as many commentators have noted, the sadness of Jer 31:15 stands out because almost every other verse in Jer 31 is about salvation. It begins with the promise, "At that time, says the LORD, I will be the God of all the families of Israel, and they shall be my people" (31:1) and refers back to God's faithfulness to Israel in the wilderness (31:2–3). It uses the imagery of gathering Israel like a flock (31:10) and bringing rest to the weary (31:25), before focusing on the "new covenant" (31:31), where God will "forgive their

---

20. "The LORD, the God of their ancestors, sent persistently to them . . . but they kept mocking the messengers of God, despising his words, and scoffing at his prophets, until the wrath of the LORD against his people became so great that there was no remedy. Therefore he brought up against them the king of the Chaldeans, who killed their youths with the sword in the house of their sanctuary, and had no compassion on young man or young woman, the aged or the feeble; he gave them all into his hand. All the vessels of the house of God, large and small, and the treasures of the house of the LORD, and the treasures of the king and of his officials, all these he brought to Babylon. They burned the house of God, broke down the wall of Jerusalem, burned all its palaces with fire, and destroyed all its precious vessels. He took into exile in Babylon those who had escaped from the sword, and they became servants to him and to his sons until the establishment of the kingdom of Persia, to fulfill the word of the LORD by the mouth of Jeremiah, until the land had made up for its sabbaths." (2 Chr 36:15–21)

iniquity, and remember their sin no more" (31:34). It is clear that Jeremiah is important to Matthew, for his is the only gospel that explicitly mentions him by name (2:17; 16:14; 27:19), and his version of the words at the last supper ("poured out for many *for the forgiveness of sins*"—26:28) is probably an allusion to this "new covenant" passage.[21] It is therefore easy to see how the themes of Jer 31 would have appealed to Matthew. Turner concludes:

> In Jeremiah's view of the future, Rachel's mourning for her children would be consoled by Israel's return to the land and the making of a new covenant. The similar mourning of the mothers of Bethlehem also occurs in the context of hope, but the hope here is now about to be actualized through the sacrificial death and resurrection of the Messiah. (Matt. 26:27–28)[22]

On this view, the typological comparison is not the "suffering" of the two sets of mothers but the "deliverance" that follows, resulting in the establishment of a new covenant. If this is the case, then as with Hos 11:1, it is easy to see how Matthew would have regarded the deliverance that follows Bethlehem's sorrow as both an "escalation" and a "completion" of the deliverance from Babylon. This raises the question, however, of why Matthew cited the "mourning and weeping" of Jer 31:15, with its obvious parallel to the suffering of the Bethlehem mothers? Would it not have been much clearer to have pointed to one of the "deliverance" passages of Jer 31, if that was what he had in mind?[23]

There are three main answers to this question. The first depends on the principle that quotations in the New Testament are expected to evoke their surrounding context. This view is particularly associated with the work of C. H. Dodd, who demonstrated that many of the scriptural quotations in the

---

21. Mark 14:24 only has "poured out for many." However, Matthew does not go as far as Luke in explicitly speaking of the cup as "the new covenant in my blood" (Luke 22:20).

22. Turner, *Matthew*, 95.

23. This is somewhat similar to the debate about Jesus' cry from the cross in Mark 15:34 ("My God, my God, why have you forsaken me?"). The words are a quotation from Ps 22:1 and begin a long section on the suffering of the psalmist: "O my God, I cry by day" (v. 2); "All who seek me mock at me" (v. 7); "trouble is near and there is no one to help" (v. 11); "all my bones are out of joint" (v. 14); "My hands and feet have shriveled" (v. 16). However, some scholars have argued that Mark (and Jesus) would have known that the psalm ends on a positive note ("future generations will be told about the Lord, and proclaim his deliverance to a people yet unborn, saying that he has done it"— v. 30–31) and so the "forsaken" saying also carries a note of victory. Other scholars think this misses the point: Jesus utters this cry because he is identifying with the suffering of the psalmist.

New Testament come from a select number of passages, such as the stories of Abraham, Moses, and David, the prophecies of Isa 40–55, Dan 7, and Zech 9–14, and selected psalms (2, 22, 69, 110). From this, he argued that quotations in the New Testament are not to be seen as isolated proof-texts but as signposts to these key theological sections of Scripture.[24] Numerous studies have confirmed this basic insight but we should exercise caution when dealing with quotations that are not drawn from this select group of passages. The flip side of Dodd's hypothesis is that a considerable number of quotations in the New Testament are *not* taken from these key passages but are in fact unique. This is the case with all of Matthew's infancy quotations and so it cannot be assumed that Dodd's principle applies to them.

Second, although Jer 31:15 associates Rachel with Ramah and 1 Sam 10:2 envisages her tomb to the north of Jerusalem "in the territory of Benjamin," Scripture knows of another tradition that links it with Bethlehem: "So Rachel died, and she was buried on the way to Ephrath (that is, Bethlehem)" (Gen 35:19; cf. 48:7). We saw in our last chapter that the Aramaic targum expands this verse to read:

> And Rachel died, and was buried in the way to Ephrath, which is Bethlehem. And Jakob erected a pillar over the house of burying: which is the pillar of the tomb of Rachel unto this day. And Jakob proceeded and spread his tent beyond the tower of Eder, *the place from whence, it is to be, the King Meshiha will be revealed at the end of the days.* (*Tg. Ps.-J.* Gen 35:20–21)

We cannot be sure that this text was in circulation in Matthew's day but if the tradition that lies behind it was known to Matthew, then it is not difficult to see how he might have associated suffering in Bethlehem with Rachel and then to the specific text of Rachel mourning for the exiles in Jer 31:15. In fact, some scholars have argued that the connection with Jer 31:15 was already present in Matthew's source because if it had originated with him, he would surely have quoted it in the form now found in Codex A, where Ramah has been translated ("in the height") rather than transliterated as a proper noun.[25] This would have given him a text that said, "A voice is heard in the height, lamentation and bitter weeping," which would have been more appropriate than a text that mentions a place that does not otherwise figure in his narrative. On the other hand, this would be just as true for whoever

24. Dodd, *According to the Scriptures*. Dodd saw this as a contrast to the "atomistic" exegesis of contemporary Judaism and believed that it originated with Jesus' own use of Scripture.

25. So Luz, *Matthew 1–7*, 119.

74

was responsible for the source, and so Menken thinks that Matthew is simply quoting the text in the form of the Septuagint known to him.[26]

The third suggestion draws on the narrative flow of the gospel. Readers have been guided through the opening chapters of Matthew to expect a deliverance from God that exceeds what has gone before. The promise of a miraculous birth is not that Mary is barren, like Sarah and Hannah in Scripture, but is a virgin. Her child will not just deliver God's people from Egypt or Babylon but from their sins (Matt 1:21). His birth is not just a matter of joy for the family or village but for visiting magi (Matt 2:10) and is accompanied by celestial signs. Thus when readers reach Matt 2:18, they are expecting a reference to salvation and since that is not immediately apparent from the words of Jer 31:15, they are prompted to search the context of the quotation to find it.[27] It would not take them long since almost every other verse of the chapter is concerned with salvation. Indeed, one could argue that the value of quoting Jer 31:15 is that as well as being a pointer to salvation, it is a reminder that salvation is wrought through suffering. This will be true of Jesus and it will be true of his future followers. As Bob Becking puts it, what the quotation points to is the affirmation that "God's power is greater than the power of sorrow-bringing forces."[28]

On the other hand, it is difficult for a modern audience to draw inspiration from a story where God miraculously rescues Jesus but leaves the children of Bethlehem to be slaughtered. Later Christian tradition solved this by regarding the children as sharing in the sufferings of Christ and hence dying as martyrs,[29] but it is by no means obvious that this is

26. Menken, *Matthew's Bible*, 143–59. His thesis is that the majority of differences that we find between Matthew's quotations and the Septuagint manuscripts that have come down to us are not changes by Matthew to better suit his argument but were already present in a revised version of the Septuagint.

27. The academic name for this is *Relevance Theory* and particularly associated with the publications of Sperber and Wilson. They advance the principle that "relevance" is a key criterion for explaining communication and cognition. Readers are confronted with a variety of factors that influence interpretation but they will generally choose those that appear to be most relevant, that is, those that require least processing effort. Thus the quotation of Mic 5:2 (a ruler will come from Bethlehem) closely fits Matthew's storyline but the quotation of Jer 31:15 produces dissonance: why this mention of Rachel and Ramah? This then acts as a catalyst to search for a context that will make it relevant and the rest of Jer 31 provides it. See Sperber and Wilson, *Relevance: Communication and Cognition*.

28. Becking, *Between Fear and Freedom*, 206.

29. Luz (*Matthew 1–7*, 122) notes that Chrysostom's view that "nothing good would have come from them anyway, since there can be no innocent human suffering" was unusual. For Leo the Great, "they were *permitted* to die for Christ, because that is better

Matthew's view. A different explanation is put forward by Richard Erickson. He argues that the Hosea quotation shows that Jesus is not only portrayed as a new Moses but also as the representative of Israel, God's Son. Thus when Moses was in danger, he fled from Egypt to Midian, apparently leaving his fellow Hebrews to their fate (Exod 2:15). But he later "return[ed] to stand before Pharaoh, fully identified with the people of Israel, in complete solidarity with them, becoming the channel of their deliverance and restoration."[30] Of course, Jesus' return is too late for the children who have been massacred, but Erickson argues that "[t]ragic though the massacre in Bethlehem may be, it is in the end no more tragic than the death of any single human being in the history of the human race. The one who escaped at Bethlehem comes back to endure it all himself, *and to reverse it!*"[31] Thus according to Erickson, the typology is not simply "suffering" or even "suffering followed by deliverance," but something like "initial escape followed by return to win victory through suffering alongside his people." Although rather cumbersome to put into words, the advantage of Erickson's view is that the typology is focused on the roles of Moses and Israel and we have seen that this is true of much of Matthew's infancy narrative.

CONCLUSION

If we set aside the view that Hos 11:1 and Jer 31:15 are predictive prophecies, as I think we must, the major discussion is whether the typologies are simply the result of hindsight or whether there are features in the original texts that can be regarded as "foreshadowing" (but nor predicting) the events surrounding Jesus' birth. We can perhaps sharpen this question by comparing it with the way that the Qumran community used biblical language to describe their leader:

> They caused [me] to be like a ship on the deeps of the [sea] and like a fortified city before [the aggressor], [and] like a *woman in travail* with her first-born child, upon whose belly pangs have come and grievous pains, filling with anguish her child-bearing crucible. For the children have come to the throes of Death (and) she labors in her pains who bears a man. For amid the throes of Death she shall *bring forth a man-child*, and amid the pains of Hell

than living in sin," while Cyprian regarded them as martyrs.

30. Erickson, "Divine Injustice?" 21.

31. Ibid., 26. Emphasis original.

there shall spring from her child-bearing crucible a *Marvelous Mighty Counselor*; and a man shall be delivered from out of the throes. (1QH Hymn 4)

The specific title, "Marvelous Mighty Counselor," is a clear reference to Isa 9:6 ("For a child has been born for us . . . and he is named Wonderful Counselor, Mighty God, Everlasting Father, Prince of Peace"), which makes it likely that the reference to being in travail and bringing forth a man-child refers to another verse in Isaiah, namely, Isa 66:7 ("Before she travailed, she brought forth; before her pain came, she was delivered of a man child"— RV). Is the claim that Jesus "fulfills" Hos 11:1 and Jer 31:15 any stronger than the claim that the leader of the Qumran community (known as the "Teacher of Righteousness") fulfills these texts from Isaiah? It cannot be argued that Hos 11:1 and Jer 31:5 contain a greater sense of "foreshadowing" than the exalted titles of Isa 9:6 and so while a sense of "foreshadowing" might be considered a *necessary* condition for typological fulfillment, it is not a *sufficient* one.

Does it then come down to the specifics of the geography? If the Teacher of Righteousness had been taken to Egypt as a child, would Matthew have acknowledged that his claim to fulfillment was equally legitimate? To ask the question is to answer it: Matthew believed that Jesus was the Son of God who brought deliverance to God's people. He did not believe this of the Teacher of Righteousness (if he ever gave it any thought) and so the claim to fulfillment does not arise. Thus while we might say that a certain "foreshadowing" can be detected in Hos 11:1 and Jer 31:15 when read in their wider contexts, I think we have to acknowledge that it is Matthew's beliefs about Jesus that govern his exegesis. For those who share Matthew's beliefs, the parallels between what Moses and Israel did in Scripture and the events surrounding Jesus' birth are convincing. But it seems to me that what makes them convincing is not the particulars of Egypt and Ramah or even Bethlehem and Nazareth but their potential for illuminating the significance of Jesus. The danger of speaking about typological fulfillment is that the word "typological" soon gets forgotten and the texts are treated like quasi-predictions. The test of typological fulfillment is not that the connections can be objectively verified but that they prove illuminating. I do not think this necessarily reduces them to mere "examples" or "analogies." Rather, it asserts that they have the potential to bring depth and insight into the meaning and significance of Jesus, *providing* that one regards Jesus as a significant and meaningful person in the first place.

5

Born of a Virgin

INTRODUCTION

[26]In the sixth month the angel Gabriel was sent by God to a town in Galilee called Nazareth, [27]to a *virgin* engaged to a man whose name was Joseph, of the house of David. The *virgin's* name was Mary. [28]And he came to her and said, "Greetings, favored one! The Lord is with you." [29]But she was much perplexed by his words and pondered what sort of greeting this might be. [30]The angel said to her, "Do not be afraid, Mary, for you have found favor with God. [31]And now, you will conceive in your womb and bear a son, and you will name him Jesus. [32]He will be great, and will be called the Son of the Most High, and the Lord God will give to him the throne of his ancestor David. [33]He will reign over the house of Jacob forever, and of his kingdom there will be no end." [34]Mary said to the angel, *"How can this be, since I am a virgin?"* [35]The angel said to her, "The Holy Spirit will come upon you, and the power of the Most High will overshadow you; therefore the child to be born will be holy; he will be called Son of God. [36]And now, your relative Elizabeth in her old age has also conceived a son; and this is the sixth month for her who was said to be barren. [37]For nothing will be impossible with God." (Luke 1:26–37)

[18]Now the birth of Jesus the Messiah took place in this way. When his mother Mary had been engaged to Joseph, but before they lived together, *she was found to be with child from the Holy Spirit.* [19]Her husband Joseph, being a righteous man and unwilling to expose her to public disgrace, planned to dismiss her quietly.

[20]But just when he had resolved to do this, an angel of the Lord appeared to him in a dream and said, "Joseph, son of David, do not be afraid to take Mary as your wife, *for the child conceived in her is from the Holy Spirit.* [21]She will bear a son, and you are to name him Jesus, for he will save his people from their sins." [22]All this took place to fulfill what had been spoken by the Lord through the prophet: [23]*"Look, the virgin shall conceive and bear a son, and they shall name him Emmanuel,"* which means, *"God is with us."* [24]When Joseph awoke from sleep, he did as the angel of the Lord commanded him; he took her as his wife, [25]but had no marital relations with her until she had borne a son; and he named him Jesus. (Matt 1:18–25)

These are the only two passages in the New Testament that speak of the virgin birth or more accurately, the virginal conception, since there is nothing to suggest that the actual birth was unusual. The claim is that Mary became pregnant while still a virgin and not through sexual intercourse, and Matthew regards this as a fulfillment of Scripture. Luke's story probably echoes a number of biblical passages (Gen 16:11; Judg 13:3; Isa 7:14; 9:6; 2 Sam 7:14) but there is no attempt to show that Scripture is being fulfilled. Indeed, the parallel between Mary and Elizabeth (Luke 1:36–37) has led some scholars to suggest that Luke was only wishing to make the point that Mary's conception was "of God," not that it took place without a human father.[1] Readers of the NRSV text above might deduce from verse 31 ("And *now,* you will conceive") that Mary became pregnant at that moment but such an interpretation would not arise from the RSV ("And behold, you will conceive"), NJB (Look! You are to conceive") or the NIV ("You will be with child") and is contrary to the promise of verse 35 ("The Holy Spirit *will* come upon you").

The translation issue is that the Greek word *idou,* which occurs fifty-seven times in Luke, is an interjection that introduces the next element of the narrative (e.g., 1:20, 31, 36, 38, 44, 48). The RSV follows the KJV and generally renders it "behold,"[2] but most modern versions try to give a more contextual meaning. Thus when Zechariah is struck dumb because of his unbelief (1:20), the context suggests that the effect is immediate and so the word "now" is appropriate ("And *now* you will be silent and not able to speak until the day this happens"—NIV). On the other hand, the context of

1. Schaberg, *The Illegitimacy of Jesus,* 101–27.

2. Forty-one out of fifty-seven in RSV; fifty-two out of fifty-seven in KJV. The NRSV never uses the word "behold" in the New Testament.

Luke 1:36 makes it clear that Elizabeth's conception is not about to happen because she is already in her sixth month. The NIV thus translates, "*Even* Elizabeth your relative is going to have a child." The point is that immediacy is not intrinsic to the word but depends on context and since Luke 1:35 contains a future promise ("The Holy Spirit *will* come upon you"), it is clear that Luke does not envisage Mary conceiving at this precise moment.

Nevertheless, Luke does envisage the conception happening fairly soon after the angel's visit, for Elizabeth is said to be in her sixth month (1:26) and has still not given birth when Mary's pregnancy is revealed (1:41). Thus Mary must have conceived within a few months of the angelic announcement. However, the more difficult question is whether Luke envisages the conception as taking place while Mary is *still* a virgin. Three reasons are usually offered in support of this. The first is that Luke twice uses the term "virgin" (*parthenos*) to introduce Mary (1:27). The word occurs over sixty times in the LXX for an unmarried girl, as in the description of Rebecca in Gen 24:16: "The girl was very fair to look upon, a virgin, whom no man had known." However, the lack of sexual experience is not always to the fore and the word is sometimes translated "girl" or "maiden," as in Gen 34:3 ("And his soul was drawn to Dinah daughter of Jacob; he loved the girl, and spoke tenderly to her"), even though the previous verse says that he had already "seized her and lay with her by force" (34:2). Thus Luke's use of *parthenos* does not in itself suggest that she was *still* a virgin when she conceived.

Second, Mary's reply ("How can this be, since I am a virgin") suggests that Mary did not take the angel's words as referring to the time after her betrothal, when according to Jewish custom, she would move into Joseph's home.[3] Given Matthew's statement that Mary's pregnancy would lead to public disgrace (Matt 1:19), it is possible that Mary understood the angel's words to mean that she and Joseph would break their betrothal vows.[4] However, if that was her understanding, one would have expected a "why" question rather than a "how" question. Mary's reply to the angel is liter-

---

3. There are important differences between "betrothal" and what we would understand by "engagement." According to later Jewish sources, betrothal would normally take place around the age of thirteen and was legally binding: infidelity was regarded as adultery and "splitting up" was like divorce. The girl would generally remain with her parents for another year and then move into the groom's house. For further details, see Schaberg, *Illegitimacy of Jesus*, 41–62.

4. Evidence from later Jewish sources suggests that sexual abstinence during the period between betrothal and marriage was not always a requirement.

ally, "How is this, since I know not a man," using the verb "to know" in its "biblical" sense (Gen 4:1, 17). In today's language, we would say: "How can this be true since I am not in a sexual relationship?" The angel's answer is suggestive ("the Holy Spirit will come upon you") but in the light of the scriptural stories of Sarah and Hannah, it is hardly proof that a human father will not be involved.

The third reason is that when Luke introduces his genealogy in chapter 3, he says: "Jesus was about thirty years old when he began his work. He was the son (as was thought) of Joseph son of Heli" (3:23). That Joseph was understood to be Jesus' legal father can be seen from Matt 13:55 ("Is not this the carpenter's son?") and John 1:45 ("We have found him about whom Moses in the law and also the prophets wrote, Jesus son of Joseph from Nazareth"). What then does Luke mean by "as was thought?" The most natural meaning is that someone else was Jesus' father, either because Mary was unfaithful to Joseph or that she became pregnant against her will. Most scholars reject the first possibility as out of keeping with the strong morality of the passage and the second as incompatible with the angel's words, "Greetings, favored one! The Lord is with you" (Luke 1:28), which is hardly true if Mary is about to be seduced or raped. Brown also notes that the parallelism between what is said of John and what is said of Jesus leads the reader to expect an even more miraculous conception than that of the aged and barren Elizabeth. This is hardly true if someone other than Joseph was Jesus' father and so although a virginal conception would be without precedent in Jewish writings, he concludes that it is the most plausible interpretation of Luke's words.[5]

Some would wish to add a fourth reason based on the words, "The Holy Spirit will come upon you" (Luke 1:35). Clearly this could support a virginal conception but the verb here translated "come upon you" (*epercho-mai*) has no sexual connotations. For example, in Acts 1:8, Jesus promises that the Holy Spirit will "come upon" the disciples so that they are equipped to evangelize the world (see also Acts 8:24; 13:40; 14:19). It does not mean that the Holy Spirit would do the work for them; rather, they will be empowered by God to accomplish their task. This is also the meaning in Luke 1:35. Mary will be empowered by God or the Holy Spirit to conceive and give birth to one who will be called "Son of God." It is not suggesting that God or the Holy Spirit will take the place of a human father; only that Mary will be enabled to perform her role. Thus the verse does not offer additional

5. Brown, *Birth of the Messiah*, 298–309.

evidence that Luke believed in a virginal conception, though it is clearly compatible with such a view.

Is Luke intending an allusion to Isa 7:14 as he narrates his story? A literal rendering of the LXX of Isa 7:14 is: "Behold, the virgin will conceive in the womb and give birth to a son and you will call his name Emmanouel." We have already noted Luke's double mention of "virgin" in 1:27, and in 1:31 he records the angel's words as, "And *behold*, you *will* conceive *in your womb and bear a son, and you shall call his name* Jesus" (RSV). The words in italics are where the Greek is identical and so it is certainly possible that Luke intends his readers to think of Isa 7:14. On the other hand, it has been argued that his use of a different word for "conceive" and the fact that the child is called "Jesus" rather than "Emmanouel" (as it is spelt in the LXX) suggests that he does not have Isa 7:14 in mind. Are these two points convincing?

The difficulty with the first point is that there is some doubt as to the original reading of the LXX of Isa 7:14. The Hebrew text uses the adjective *hareh* ("pregnant"), which the LXX generally translates by the idiom *en gastri echei* (literally, "have in the womb") and this is accepted as the original reading of Isa 7:14 by both the leading editions of the LXX.[6] However, some important manuscripts uses the verb *lambano* ("receive"), which puts the emphasis more on conception ("receive in the womb") rather than pregnancy ("have in the womb").[7] Luke is closer to the latter but uses the compound form *sunlambano*, which is the verb the LXX generally uses for conceiving.[8] Since the LXX never uses *sunlambano* in conjunction with *en gastri*, it could be argued that Luke is following his own style and is not pointing to Isa 7:14. On the other hand, Luke uses *sunlambano* to describe Elizabeth's conception (1:24) and may have added *en gastri* in 1:31 because he did have Isa 7:14 in mind.

As for the second point, Matthew has a very similar statement in 1:21 ("She will bear a son, and you are to name him Jesus"), but then goes on

6. The most popular edition of the LXX was edited by Alfred Rahlfs in 1935 and is the version usually found in Bible programs such as Logos and Bibleworks. Its weakness is that its text was largely constructed on the basis of just three manuscripts, Sinaiticus (fourth century C.E.), Vaticanus (fourth century C.E.), and Alexandrinus (fifth century C.E.). The other edition is known as the Göttingen series (from its place of publication) and takes into account a far greater number of manuscripts, though it is not available for every book of the LXX.

7. Menken (*Matthew's Bible*, 121–24) argues that this was the original reading because: (1) It is more likely that scribes would be tempted to change *lambano* to the more usual *echo*; and (2) They would be tempted to conform Isa 7:14 to Matt 1:23.

8. E.g., Gen 4:1, 17; 16:4; 19:36; 21:2; 25:21; 29:32, 33, 34, 35.

to cite Isa 7:14 in full, along with an explanation that "Emmanouel" means "God is with us" (1:23). Again, one could argue that if Luke had Isa 7:14 in mind, he would surely have wanted to make something of the term "Emmanouel," but this is an argument from silence. As we shall see later, Matthew has his own reasons for emphasizing the abiding presence of God/Jesus with his people but this theme is less prominent in Luke. Thus he may simply have thought that explaining the meaning of "Emmanouel" at this point in his narrative would only complicate matters (as some readers might be thinking about my previous paragraph). Brown thinks the question must be left open but Nolland finds it difficult to accept that Luke had Isa 7:14 in mind.[9] Before we consider Matthew's explicit use of the text, we will first look at the context of the verse in the book of Isaiah.

ISAIAH 7:14 IN CONTEXT

[1]In the days of Ahaz son of Jotham son of Uzziah, king of Judah, King Rezin of Aram and King Pekah son of Remaliah of Israel went up to attack Jerusalem. . . . [2]When the house of David heard . . . the heart of Ahaz and the heart of his people shook as the trees of the forest shake before the wind. [3]Then the LORD said to Isaiah, "Go out to meet Ahaz, you and your son Shear-jashub, . . . [4]and say to him, 'Take heed, be quiet, do not fear, and do not let your heart be faint because of these two smoldering stumps of firebrands, because of the fierce anger of Rezin and Aram and the son of Remaliah. . . . [11]Ask a sign of the LORD your God; let it be deep as Sheol or high as heaven.'" [12]But Ahaz said, "I will not ask, and I will not put the LORD to the test." [13]Then Isaiah said: "Hear then, O house of David! Is it too little for you to weary mortals, that you weary my God also? [14]Therefore the Lord himself will give you a sign. Look, the young woman is with child and shall bear a son, and shall name him Immanuel. [15]He shall eat curds and honey by the time he knows how to refuse the evil and choose the good. [16]For before the child knows how to refuse the evil and choose the good, the land before whose two kings you are in dread *will* be deserted. [17]The LORD will bring on you and on your people and on your ancestral house such days as have not come since the day that Ephraim departed from Judah— the king of Assyria." (Isa 7:1–4, 11–17)

9. Brown, *Birth of the Messiah*, 300; Nolland, *Luke 1—9:20*, 51.

If this is a faithful rendering of the Hebrew text, it is clearly not a prediction of a virginal conception or indeed of anything in the distant future. Verse 16 links back to verse 1 and the threat to Jerusalem posed by an alliance between Syria (Rezin) and Israel (Pekah), which can be dated to 734 B.C.E. Isaiah's word to Ahaz is that a "young woman is with child" and before the child has the moral capacity to distinguish good from evil, the threat will be over. Unlike Jer 31:15 and Hos 11:1, the text is indeed a prophecy ("*will be deserted*") but its fulfilment lies within the near future. If we ask who this child might be, the son born to Isaiah in the next chapter (8:3) is the most likely candidate, for he is linked with the term "Immanuel" (8:8), is specifically called a "sign" (8:18), and the threat posed by Rezin and Pekah will have disappeared "before the child knows how to call 'My father' or 'My mother'" (8:4). Although this metaphor suggests a couple of years, whereas distinguishing between good and evil points to an age of twelve or so, the general import is the same: the threat posed by Rezin and Pekah will soon be over. As Brown says:

> The sign offered by the prophet was the imminent birth of a child, probably Davidic, but naturally conceived, who would illustrate God's providential care for his people. The child would help preserve the House of David and would thus signify that God was still "with us."[10]

It is not difficult to see how such a prophecy could be interpreted typologically. The birth of a child is a fairly obvious sign of new life and in the context of a conquered nation, could easily point to future deliverance. Since Matthew believes that Jesus will deliver God's people from their sins (1:21), he would no doubt have thought of this as an "even greater deliverance" than what Isaiah predicted. Isaiah had a "young woman" in mind (perhaps his wife), who would shortly give birth to a son and this would be a sign of Jerusalem's deliverance from the "two smoldering stumps of firebrands." For Matthew, it would have seemed obvious that this "prefigures" the even greater deliverance brought about by the conception and birth of Jesus. If Matthew is only thinking of (what we would call) typological fulfillment, then the claim is not particularly controversial.

Before we consider this, there is more to be said about the Isaiah passage. Firstly, there is the question of the translation of Isa 7:14, as can be seen from the following:

10. Brown, *Birth of the Messiah*, 148.

Behold, a *virgin* shall conceive, and bear a son, and shall call his name Immanuel [KJV].

The *virgin* will be with child and will give birth to a son, and will call him Immanuel [NIV].

Behold, a *young woman* shall conceive and bear a son, and shall call his name Immanuel [RSV].

Look, the *young woman* is with child and shall bear a son, and shall name him Immanuel [NRSV].

The first issue is the translation of the Hebrew word *almah*. Most scholars agree that its general meaning is "young woman" and it rather looks like the choice of "virgin" by the KJV was theologically motivated. On the other hand, if we look at the six other occurrences of the word in the Hebrew Bible,[11] the KJV uses "virgin" for three of them (Gen 24:43; Song 1:3; 6:8), and so this suspicion does not appear to be justified. Most modern translations use "young woman" in Isa 7:14 but the NIV sides with the KJV and also uses "virgin" for Song 6:8. More significantly, the LXX translator used the specific word for virgin (*parthenos*) in Gen 24:43 and Isa 7:14 and *neanis* ("young girl") or *neotes* ("youth") in the others. So while the Hebrew word tends to emphasize youth rather than virginity, it would appear that context can sometimes suggest that "virgin" is an appropriate translation.[12]

The second issue follows on from this, for if the meaning of *almah* in Isa 7:14 is "virgin" and the adjective *hareh* means "pregnant," then we appear to have a virginal conception in the eighth century B.C.E. This is because there is no connecting word between the noun "virgin" and the adjective "pregnant" in the Hebrew text, so the most likely translation is, "Behold, the virgin *is* pregnant." Such a meaning is avoided in the NRSV because it renders *almah* with "young woman" and so the translation, "the young woman is with child," means that someone is currently pregnant and will in the near future give birth to a son. It cannot therefore refer to Isaiah's son, whose conception is narrated in Isa 8:3 ("And I went to the prophetess, and she conceived and bore a son").

For those translations that render *almah* with "virgin" (including the LXX), a future tense is adopted from the rest of the sentence and hence, "The virgin *will* be with child and *will* give birth to a son, and *will* call

11. Gen 24:43; Exod 2:8; Ps 68:25; Prov 30:19; Song 1:3; 6:8; Isa 7:14.

12. It is not that *almah* can only mean "young girl" and *parthenos* can only mean "virgin"; it is a matter of emphasis.

him Immanuel" (NIV). However, because the conception now lies in the future, we would need a strong indication in the text that the conception is to be understood as taking place without a human father. Indeed, we do not know of any Jewish writing which understood Isa 7:14 as involving anything but a normal conception. It is also unlikely that Isaiah's wife is in mind, for she has already borne him a child (Shear-jashub) and is not, therefore, a virgin.[13] Justin knows of a Jewish tradition that identified the child with Hezekiah, probably because of his prominence in Isa 36–39 and his reputation as a reforming king. However, 2 Kgs 18:2 speaks against this, as Hezekiah is said to be aged twenty-five at his accession and was therefore born at least six years before this promise.

A further difficulty with the passage is that verse 17 ("The LORD will bring on you . . . the king of Assyria") and what follows in verses 18–25 suggests that hardship rather than deliverance is in mind. Yes, Rezin and Pekah will be destroyed but life under Assyrian rule will be no picnic: "On that day every place where there used to be a thousand vines, worth a thousand shekels of silver, will become briers and thorns" (Isa 7:23). Of course, one could argue that servitude is better than annihilation but it is hard to see how it constitutes "deliverance." Thus the meaning of Isaiah's prophecy is obscure, not to say enigmatic, and this may have contributed to the idea that its ultimate fulfillment lies in the distant future.

Another factor that might have contributed to such a view is the notion of "sign." When Isaiah tells Ahaz that he can ask for a sign, he is told that it can be as "deep as Sheol or high as heaven." Although he refuses to ask for such a sign, probably because he has already decided on an alliance with Assyria rather than trusting in God, he is given one anyway, and it is not unreasonable to interpret it in such grandiose terms. Thus it could be argued that a sign that is as "deep as Sheol or high as heaven" points beyond the immediate context and if this is combined with the extraordinary name *Immanuel*,[14] which means, "God (is) with us," a case can be made for some

13. Although it is possible that Isa 8:3 ("And I went to the prophetess, and she conceived and bore a son") could refer to a different woman than the mother of Shear-jashub, perhaps because she had died.

14. The Hebrew name *Immanuel* consists of the preposition "with" (*im*) combined with the suffix for "us" (*nu*) and the ordinary word for God (*el*). It occurs again in Isa 8:8 ("its outspread wings will fill the breadth of your land, O Immanuel") but in Isa 8:10, it is part of ordinary speech ("it will not stand, for God is with us"). The LXX translates the term in Isa 8:8 and 10 but transliterates it in Isa 7:14 as Emmanouel. It is doubtful that a Greek speaker would understand the name Emmanouel to mean "God with us," hence the need for an explanation in Matt 1:23.

sort of miraculous intervention. Indeed, it may suggest that it should be connected with the promised son in Isa 9:6–7:

> For a child has been born for us, a son given to us; authority rests upon his shoulders; and he is named Wonderful Counselor, Mighty God, Everlasting Father, Prince of Peace. His authority shall grow continually, and there shall be endless peace for the throne of David and his kingdom. He will establish and uphold it with justice and with righteousness from this time onward and forevermore. (Isa 9:6–7)

It is still difficult to see how this specifically points to a conception without a human father but the exalted language ("Mighty God, Everlasting Father") could suggest something beyond the normal. Is Matthew's assertion that Isa 7:14 was fulfilled in the virginal conception of Jesus a credible interpretation of this line of thinking?

MATTHEW'S USE OF ISAIAH 7:14

If the meaning of Isa 7:14 is somewhat obscure, there does not appear to be any doubt as to how Matthew understood it. He begins by telling us that Mary became pregnant while betrothed to Joseph "but before they came together" (1:18). This is probably a reference to the time when Mary would leave the family home and move in with Joseph, though "came together" could have a sexual connotation. The point is reiterated at the end of the narrative, when Joseph takes Mary as his wife "but had no marital relations with her until[15] she had borne a son" (1:25). This denial that Joseph is Jesus' natural father is paralleled by two references to the conception being "from the Holy Spirit" (1:18, 20). Thus whatever the original meaning of Isa 7:14, it appears that Matthew understood it as a prophecy of a future virginal conception and he claims that this was fulfilled in Jesus.

Matthew prepares for the quotation by echoing its language in the preceding narrative. Thus the phrase, "to be with child" (Matt 1:18), uses the same idiom as the LXX of Isa 7:14 (lit. "having in the womb"),[16] while the words in Matt 1:21 ("She will bear a son, and you are to name him") reproduce the Greek of Isa 7:14 exactly. The effect is to increase the cor-

15. There has been much debate as to whether the word "until" implies that he did have sexual relations after the birth of Jesus, which has tended to be the Protestant view. The Roman Catholic view is that Mary remained a virgin all her life.

16. Or at least one part of the tradition; other manuscripts have "receive in the womb."

relation between event and quotation but it also highlights an important difference: the child was not named "Emmanuel," as in Isa 7:14, but "Jesus" (Matt 1:21, 25):

> *All this* took place to fulfill what had been spoken by the *Lord* through the prophet: "Look, the virgin shall conceive and bear a son, and *they* shall name him Emmanuel," which means, "God is with us." (Matt 1:22–23)

Most commentators believe that the explanation for this lies in a change of wording from Isa 7:14 (Hebrew and LXX). The original uses a second person singular ("*you* shall name") but Matthew has a third person plural ("*they* shall name"). In English, this remains puzzling but the Greek verb "to name" also means "to call" and so Matthew's text refers to an unspecified group of people who will call the child Emmanuel, which means, "God is with us." This is often then linked with two other texts in Matthew's Gospel, which speak about the abiding presence of God/Jesus:

> For where two or three are gathered in my name, *I am there among them.* (Matt 18:20)

> Go therefore and make disciples of all nations, baptizing them in the name of the Father and of the Son and of the Holy Spirit, and teaching them to obey everything that I have commanded you. And remember, *I am with you always,* to the end of the age. (Matt 28:19–20)

If this is correct, then the fulfillment of this aspect of Isa 7:14 does not lie in the actual naming of Jesus but how he will come to be viewed by his followers. It is surely no coincidence that the Gospel of Matthew begins with a promise of God's presence and ends with the claim that Jesus will be with his disciples "to the end of the age." Jesus is the promised "Emmanuel," not because this was his name but because he mediates the presence of God. According to Matthew, God calls Jesus "Son" at his baptism (3:17) and has Jesus say that, "no one knows the Father except the Son and anyone to whom the Son chooses to reveal him" (11:27). If Matthew wants a text to support this, then Isa 7:14 is a good choice, for it promises the birth of a child who will be called "Emmanuel," which means, "God is with us." All he had to do was change *kaleseis* ("you shall name/call") to *kalesousin* ("they shall name/call").

As with the previous quotations, some will find it difficult to accept that Matthew's readers would have found this convincing given that he has had to modify the text to make his point. We have already suggested several answers to this objection but there are two features of Matthew's introduction to the text that might be relevant in this case. Firstly, he begins with the words, "*All this* took place to fulfill . . ." This could suggest that the purpose of the quotation is not so much to prove the virginal conception but to show that everything that is happening is part of the divine plan that God would one day dwell with his people (Lev 26:12; Ezek 37:27; Zech 2:10). This was encapsulated in the promise of the child called "Emmanuel," though the context of Isa 7:14 made the identification of this child difficult. Matthew believes that the promised child is Jesus and also knows traditions that his conception was "from the Holy Spirit" (Matt 1:18, 20). Isaiah 7:14 was therefore an apt verse to quote and the fact that the LXX rendered the Hebrew *almah* with *parthenos* ("virgin") was a bonus.

Second, the text is introduced as, "spoken by the Lord through the prophet." Now this could simply be an acknowledgement that it was the Lord who commanded Isaiah to speak to Ahaz but perhaps there is something else, namely, that Matthew was aware that his quotation differs from what is written in Isaiah. In other words, Matthew believed that he was offering the divine meaning of the text, the meaning *the Lord* intended but not necessarily understood by Isaiah. We today would indicate this in a series of hermeneutical steps but in Matthew's day, it was common practice to combine them by offering a modified quotation. The insertion of the "by no means" into the Bethlehem quotation is the clearest example in Matthew, because the change from "least" to "by no means least" was hardly intended to deceive. The change from "you will call" to "they will call" is only slightly less obvious.

There is an alternative explanation for the third person plural "they will name/call," namely, that this was simply the form that Matthew found in his text. Maarten Menken has shown that some of the differences between Matthew's quotations and the LXX manuscripts that have come down to us are difficult to understand as deliberate changes. They do not make a point that would enhance Matthew's argument or necessarily conform to his style. In the case of Isa 7:14, he disputes the view that Matthew would have seen a contradiction between the names "Jesus" and "Emmanuel," as if the meaning, "he will save his people from their sins" was applicable at his birth but "God is with us" only later, once he had gained followers. He also notes that the Hebrew manuscript designated 1QIsaᵃ found at Qumran has a third person singular ending, probably to be understood as an impersonal, "one will call." He concludes that Matthew knew a text of Isa 7:14 that used a third person plural and he quotes it, without any sense that it contradicts the fact that the child was called Jesus. Such a contradiction, he says, lies only in the minds of modern scholars.[17]

IS A VIRGINAL CONCEPTION BELIEVABLE?

Many Christians would answer this question by quoting the words of the angel to Mary in Luke 1:37: "For nothing will be impossible to God." If scientists point out that Jesus would not have the requisite chromosomes without a human father, the response is: "For mortals it is impossible, but for God all things are possible" (Matt 19:26). However, we have already seen that at least one element of the birth narrative cannot be taken literally (a star that can point out a particular house) and so perhaps the same is true of the virginal conception. Is it a symbolic story designed to illustrate the truth that Jesus' conception and birth are "from the Holy Spirit" and is not meant to be taken literally? After all, no one takes this phrase to mean that the Holy Spirit supplied the seed to make Mary pregnant. So why take the rest of the story literally?

The obvious answer to this is that Matthew appears to take it literally but then the same could be said for the "sat-nav" star and also for the events that are said to have accompanied the crucifixion:

> Then Jesus cried again with a loud voice and breathed his last. At that moment the curtain of the temple was torn in two, from top to bottom. The earth shook, and the rocks were split. The tombs also were opened, *and many bodies of the saints who had fallen asleep were raised.* After his resurrection they came out of the tombs and entered the holy city and appeared to many. (Matt 27:50–53)

This story is written in the same matter-of-fact style as the infancy narrative but many scholars regard it as symbolic: Jesus' resurrection is not an isolated incident but marks the beginning of the general resurrection. There are two main reasons for this. First, it is not mentioned in any of the other gospels or in any other source. If "many" people were reunited with their loved ones shortly after Jesus' death, it would surely have been noted somewhere. Second, given Matthew's emphasis on the fulfillment of Scripture, this looks like a fulfillment of Ezek 37:13: "And you shall know that I am the LORD, when I open your graves, and bring you up from your graves, O my people." Readers in the first century, it is argued, would not have read Matthew's narrative and gone looking for their past relatives; they would have intuitively realized that it is making a theological point about the significance of Jesus' death and resurrection. The question then is whether the same might be true of the virginal conception?

There is of course a significant difference in that the resurrection story only alludes to a scriptural passage, whereas the virginal conception is supported by a specific proof-text. However, this raises the question of whether the proof-text has generated the story rather than the story prompting the proof-text. We have seen in previous chapters that this is unlikely to be the case for Hos 11:1 or Jer 31:15, as they are not prophecies in their original context. It is possible that the future promise of Mic 5:2 ("from you *shall* come forth for me one who is to rule in Israel") could have generated the Bethlehem stories, especially Luke's (mis)timing of the census, though this remains a matter of debate.

The case for Isa 7:14 generating the virginal conception of Jesus depends on how that text was understood. If it was understood to be speaking of a virginal conception in the future, as some conservative scholars maintain, then one can see how the early church might have assumed that it applies to Jesus, whether they had any specific evidence for it or not. Put another way, given their beliefs about Jesus, they would hardly have thought that it applies to anyone else. On the other hand, most scholars do not regard Isa 7:14 as predicting a virginal conception and there is not a single Jewish document that expects the Messiah to be born of a virgin. Thus according to Evans, it is much more likely that Matthew knew traditions about the virginal conception and was led to Isa 7:14 in order to explain them.[18]

Of course, this does not mean that the traditions themselves were historically reliable. Perhaps a virginal conception was invented not to specifically fulfill Isa 7:14 but to show that Jesus is greater than any of the heroes and gods of contemporary religion. For example, the conception of Perseus, Romulus, Alexander, and Augustus were all believed to be miraculous. If the Christians wanted to claim that Jesus was the true Lord, greater and mightier than any of these figures, then he would need a birth story more miraculous than those attributed to them. However, these stories usually involve a god coming down and impregnating a woman and thus giving birth to a special person. Brown argues that the early Christians would have found such stories morally repugnant and would hardly have attempted to emulate them. One could perhaps argue that the virginal conception was an attempt to remove the "pagan" element from these stories, but if this was the case, it is surprising that he speaks of conception "from the Holy Spirit," which would almost certainly be taken as divine impregnation. The

18. Evans, *Matthew*, 63.

91

emphasis on the purity and blamelessness of Mary and Joseph makes it unlikely that the virginal conception is based on "impregnation" myths.[19]

A more likely scenario is the theory offered by Roger Aus. He thinks the inspiration for the virginal conception, like so much of the infancy narratives, is to be found in Jewish traditions concerning the birth of Moses. For example, when Pharaoh ordered all the male children to be thrown into the Nile (Exod 2:22), there is a tradition that states that Amram divorced his wife Jochebed, so that this fate would not befall their children. However, Miriam persuaded him that this course of action would lead Israel to lose their female children also and was therefore worse than Pharaoh's decree. Amram thus vowed to take back Jochebed "quietly" but when this was put to the Sanhedrin,[20] he was urged to do it publicly as an example to the people. Aus thinks that this is the inspiration behind Joseph wanting to divorce Mary "quietly" but was then persuaded by the angel to take her (openly) as his wife.

However, Aus' main point is that Jochebed's ability to conceive Moses in her old age was regarded as a miracle, for the "signs of maidenhood" returned to her. She became a "youth" again and Aus regards the Aramaic term as equivalent to the Hebrew *almah*. Although we are not talking about a virginal conception, as Amram is regarded as the father of Moses, the miracle is that having already borne Miriam and Aaron, Jochebed's virginity was miraculously restored. He notes that similar things are said about Sarah's conception of Isaac in her old age and it is these traditions that provided the inspiration for the virginal conception of Jesus. It is a "typically Jewish Christian haggadic embellishment of the birth of Israel's final redeemer," based on stories of the birth of Israel's first redeemer.[21] It is not "historical" in the modern sense of the word, but it does convey "religious truth" in a form that would have been convincing at the time. Aus completely denies that any form of deception is involved; it was the most natural way for a Jewish Christian like Matthew to express the profound truth that Jesus is "Israel's final redeemer."[22]

---

19. Brown, *Birth of the Messiah*, 517–33.

20. This anachronism is typical of such writings. The Jewish council known in the first century as the Sanhedrin is read back into the narratives about Moses.

21. Aus, *Matthew 1–2*, 84.

22. Crossan and Borg agree: "Our conclusion is that Matthew very, very deliberately based Jesus' conception closely on the midrashic versions of Moses's conception already current in the first century" (109).

Another possible source for the virginal conception is Philo. In *Cher* 40–52 (XII–XV), Philo draws a distinction between natural conception, which gives birth to the physical, and divine conception, which gives birth to "the virtues." As is often the case with Philo, it is difficult to ascertain whether his allegorical interpretations bypass the literal meaning of the texts or build on them. Consider the following antithesis between human and divine begetting:

> A husband unites with his wife, and the male human being with the female human being in a union which tends to the generation of children, in strict accordance with and obedience to nature. But it is not lawful for virtues, which are the parents of many perfect things, to associate with a mortal husband. But they, without having received the power of generation from any other being, will never be able by themselves alone to conceive anything. Who, then, is it who sows good seed in them, except the Father of the universe, the uncreated God, he who is the parent of all things? (*Cher* 43–44)

On its own, one would assume that Philo is talking about the begetting of "ideas" and thus has no relevance to an actual virginal conception. Notice, for example, the reference to the "soul" in the following quotation: "For the association of men, with a view to the procreation of children, makes virgins women. *But when God begins to associate with the soul,* he makes that which was previously woman now again virgin" (50a). However, this divine "association" is closely tied to the *actual* conceptions of Sarah (45), Leah (46), and Rebecca (47), and he specifically says of Rebecca that "when the all-wise Isaac addressed his supplications to God, Rebecca, who is perseverance, *became pregnant by the agency of him who received the supplication*" (47). It is unlikely that Philo is intending to deny the human role of Isaac in Rebecca's conception but it is secondary to the divine begetting required to produce "the virtues." Although the thought-world is very different, it is possible that the early church thought a "divine begetting" was equally necessary to produce the "Son of God."[23]

---

23. So Aus, *Matthew 1–2*, 61–63. Brown speaks of it as a "serious possibility" but nevertheless concludes that "we remain without real proof of the existence in Judaism of that idea of a virginal conception that might have influenced Jewish Christians in their thinking about Jesus" (*Birth of the Messiah*, 524). However, Lincoln ("Contested Paternity," 223) thinks this misses the point. Philo's "discussions indicate clearly that the notion of God impregnating a virgin was readily available to him, presumably from his acquaintance with Egyptian and Graeco-Roman legends" and that he can "employ this

Moving in a completely different direction, it has been suggested that the virginal conception was an attempt to defend Jesus from the charge of illegitimacy. Both Tertullian and Origen in the second century had to defend Jesus from such a charge and it is possible that it lies behind the dialogue found in John 8. Jesus is claiming that God is his father and accuses his hearers of not recognizing this because they do not know God.

> "I testify on my own behalf, and the Father who sent me testifies on my behalf." Then they said to him, *"Where is your Father?"* Jesus answered, "You know neither me nor my Father. If you knew me, you would know my Father also." . . . They answered him, "Abraham is our father." Jesus said to them, "If you were Abraham's children, you would be doing what Abraham did, but now you are trying to kill me, a man who has told you the truth that I heard from God. This is not what Abraham did. You are indeed doing what your father does." They said to him, *"We are not illegitimate children*; we have one father, God himself." (John 8:18–19, 39–41)

The dialogue can be understood solely in terms of God as the father, but it is possible that their initial question ("Where is your father?") contains a personal challenge, because they know that Jesus cannot produce one. Similarly, their denial ("We are not illegitimate children") could contain an unspoken, "unlike you," especially as a literal rendering of the Greek is, "We were not born of fornication" (RSV). Misunderstanding between "earthly things" and "heavenly things" is common in John's Gospel (3:12; 4:11; 6:52), so it is difficult to be sure that an accusation of illegitimacy is present, but it is accepted by a number of commentators.[24]

The other piece of New Testament evidence is the unusual designation of Jesus in Mark 6:3 ("the carpenter, the son of Mary"). The fact that Matthew has "the son of the carpenter" (13:55) and Luke has "the son of Joseph" (4:22) could suggest that they found Mark's designation objectionable, and indeed some manuscripts of Mark 6:3 also read "son of the carpenter." One explanation for this is that Joseph died soon after the birth of Jesus, and so Jesus was known in the village as the "son of Mary," but this does not explain why later writers and scribes were so eager to change it. Although the evidence is slight, it does appear that rumors of illegitimacy were current in Jesus' day.

---

notion in the interpretation of the Jewish Scriptures."

24. Smith, *John*, 189; Barrett, *Gospel according to St John*, 288. Brown (*Birth of the Messiah*, 542) says the matter must be left open.

Schaberg accepts this tradition but does not think that Matthew and Luke turned it into a story of a virginal conception; that was the work of the later church. If Matthew and Luke are read in the light of Scripture and not later church doctrine, readers are far more likely to interpret the story as God bringing deliverance from disaster rather than an unprecedented suspension of nature. For example, the function of the four women in the genealogy is that they are all "wronged or thwarted by the male world,"[25] yet miraculously protected by God. The story of a young girl conceiving a child without a human father (and without the pain of childbirth, according to later tradition) is hardly a parallel to their situation, but a girl who has been violated while betrothed to another man, fits very well. It is the natural meaning of Luke's statement that Joseph was only "thought" to be Jesus' father and explains the parallel with her relative Elizabeth, who exclaims: "This is what the Lord has done for me when he looked favorably on me and took away the *disgrace* I have endured among my people" (Luke 1:25). The even greater "miracle" for Mary is not a virginal conception, as Brown insists, but protection and deliverance from an even greater disgrace, namely, rape. It also explains the use of *tapeinosis* in Mary's song (Luke 1:48), which should probably be translated as, "he has looked upon the *humiliation* of his servant." The NRSV's use of "lowliness" and the NIV's use of "humble estate" turns it into a virtue to be rewarded ("Surely, from now on all generations will call me blessed") rather than a humiliation that has been overcome.

To support this view, Schaberg notes that there is a close verbal link between Luke's description of Mary as a "virgin engaged to a man" (1:27) and the laws concerning a "young woman, a virgin already engaged to be married" in Deut 22:23–29.[26] The laws aim to clarify the difference between seduction and rape and in verse 29, the perpetrator is said to have "violated" (*tapeinoo*) the young girl. This then provides the background for understanding Luke's narrative and in particular, Mary's song, which gives thanks for God's *mercy* (Luke 1:50), a strange term to use for a miraculous conception. We have already seen that read on its own terms, the evidence for a virginal conception in Luke's account is marginal, but most commentators assume that Matthew's explicit quotation of Isa 7:14 makes it certain for his gospel and thus tilts the balance for Luke also. However, given that Isa 7:14 was not referring to a virginal conception in its original context

25. Schaberg, *Illegitimacy*, 32.

26. The Greek of Luke 1:27 (*parthenon emnesteumenen andri*) is almost identical to the LXX of Deut 22:23 (*parthenon memnesteumene andri*).

95

and was not interpreted as such by any later writer, Schaberg questions this assumption. Is it not more likely, she asks, that Matthew understood Isa 7:14 as a sign of God's deliverance from an imminent threat, which fits remarkably well with Mary's situation (violated while betrothed)? Thus if Matthew's readers had heard rumors that Jesus was illegitimate, they would most likely have understood his narrative in this way:

> When his mother Mary had been engaged to Joseph, but before they lived together, *she was violated,* but the child she carried was from the Holy Spirit. Her husband Joseph, being a righteous man and unwilling to expose her to public disgrace, planned to dismiss her quietly. But just when he had resolved to do this, an angel of the Lord appeared to him in a dream and said, "Joseph, son of David, do not be afraid to take Mary as your wife *even though you are not the father,* for the child conceived in her is from the Holy Spirit. She will bear a son, and you are to name him Jesus, for he will save his people from their sins." All this took place to fulfill what had been spoken by the Lord through the prophet: "Look, the virgin shall conceive and bear a son, and they shall name him Emmanuel," which means, "God is with us."[27]

Is this a plausible understanding of the infancy stories? It clearly makes sense of some of the details (women in the genealogy; overcoming Elizabeth's disgrace; God's mercy to Mary; Joseph not the father) and offers a more straightforward interpretation of Matthew's quotation of Isa 7:14. Far from taking it out of context or importing an unprecedented virginal conception into the meaning of the words, Matthew is simply asserting that the conception and birth of a child has led to an even greater deliverance (and perhaps also judgment) than in Isaiah's day. In that sense, it is consistent with the other quotations, where the consequences of Jesus leaving Egypt and Herod's slaughter of the young children are said to fulfill Hos 11:1 and Jer 31:15 respectively. That it contradicts nearly two thousand years of church doctrine will be a stumbling block for many but Schaberg insists that this must be balanced by the actual arguments used in the early church to support it. For example, few people today will find Tertullian's logic convincing:

> Christ cannot lie. He said he was the son of man. Therefore he had a human parent. But God was his father. Therefore Mary, his

---

27. It should be noted that Schaberg does not paraphrase the passage like this; it is my attempt to convey how she thinks it would have been understood.

mother, was the human parent. But if so, she was a virgin. Otherwise he had two fathers, a divine and a human one, the thought of which is ridiculous, like the stories of Castor and Hercules. Moreover, the prophecy of Isaiah is alone fulfilled by the exclusion of a human father and the acceptance of the virginity of Mary.[28]

On the other hand, it is difficult to reconcile a forthcoming rape with the angel's words in Luke 1:28 ("Greetings, *favored* one! The Lord is with you") and Luke 1:30 ("Do not be afraid, Mary, for you have *found favor* with God"), or indeed Mary's consent in Luke 1:38 ("let it be with me according to your word"). Schaberg responds to the latter by saying that Mary consents "in ignorance of her specific fate, but in trust that she will be empowered and protected by God,"[29] but Luke's use of "favored/found favor" remains a difficulty. It is also to be noted that rumors of illegitimacy (John 8:41) are not necessarily evidence for Schaberg's position, for they are equally explainable on the theory of a virginal conception (i.e., Mary gave birth rather soon after she and Joseph began living together). Indeed, Paul's statement in Gal 4:4 ("born of a woman, born under the law"), which is often used to show that he was unaware of a "virginal conception" tradition, also states that Jesus was born "under the law." Brown suggests that Paul would hardly have said this if he thought Jesus was in fact illegitimate.[30] Indeed, if Schaberg is correct that Luke intended to portray an illegitimate conception, Brown concludes that Luke must be regarded as incompetent, for it went unnoticed for nearly 2,000 years, and even now that it has been "discovered," most scholars still find it difficult to recognize. If it is possible to talk of a consensus on such a controversial matter, it is probably this: the historical evidence for a virginal conception is very thin, but none of the alternative theories are especially convincing.[31]

---

28. Tertullian, *Against Marcion* 4:10, cited in Schaberg, *Illegitimacy,* 188.

29. Schaberg, *Illegitimacy,* 138.

30. Brown, *Birth of the Messiah,* 697–712.

31. Ibid., 527. Bruner (*Matthew*, 43) says, "if the counterarguments are so often bizarre, why not take a relatively modest leap of faith and believe that Matthew and Luke—our only two documentary witnesses—are giving us what they claim to be giving us: credible accounts of Jesus' birth?" Of course, for those who reject the virginal conception, like Bishop Spong, this is not a "modest" leap but a descent into irrationalism.

CONCLUSION

Since there are significant debates about the meaning of Isa 7:14 in its original context, as well as the precise meaning of the infancy narratives of Matthew and Luke, I will begin by outlining four possible answers to the question of this chapter:

1. Isa 7:14 was referring to a future virginal conception and this was fulfilled when Mary conceived by the Holy Spirit without a human father.

2. Isa 7:14 was not referring to a future virginal conception but was typologically fulfilled when Mary conceived by the Holy Spirit without a human father.

3. Isa 7:14 was not referring to a future virginal conception but was typologically fulfilled when Mary conceived (by Joseph or someone else) but was "overshadowed" by the Holy Spirit and became a sign of an even greater deliverance.

4. Isa 7:14 was not referring to a future virginal conception, Jesus was not born of a virgin and it has been a mistake to speak about "fulfillment."

The first has been the traditional view in the church but this meaning of Isa 7:14 has always been disputed by Jewish commentators and biblical scholarship now largely agrees. Earlier debates focused on the meaning of the Hebrew word *almah* and its translation as *parthenos* in the LXX, but today the issue is more to do with historical context. It is difficult to avoid the "plain" sense of the words in Isa 7:14–16 that the passage is speaking about a child in the eighth century B.C.E. and a future deliverance before he reaches maturity. If Isaiah had in mind a birth some eight centuries later, then his message to Ahaz was cruelly misleading. Many scholars would wish to argue that this does not necessarily exhaust Isaiah's meaning but nevertheless agree that its primary meaning is referring to an event in the eighth century B.C.E.

The second view is popular and depends on the flexibility of the term "typological." For example, Blomberg uses the idea of "double fulfillment" to suggest that the text was fulfilled in Isaiah's generation but the "larger, eschatological context, especially of Isa. 9:1–7,"[32] points forward to a more complete fulfillment in Jesus. Hagner speaks of a "secondary level of meaning," which was prompted by two things: the significance of the name

---

32. Blomberg, "Matthew," 5.

Emmanuel and the promise of a "golden age" in Isaiah 9 and 11 (and 2:2–4). This is what prompted the LXX translator to use the specific word *parthenos,* because he understood the text to have "supernatural associations."[33] Keener says that because Isaiah spoke of the child as a sign, Matthew was right to recognize "in Immanuel (cf. Isa 8:8) a sign pointing to the ultimate presence of God and triumph for Judah in the Davidic Messiah who would be born to Israel."[34] All three would agree that it is appropriate to speak of this aspect of Jesus' birth as a "fulfillment" of Scripture.

The third view consists of those who think of Jesus as either illegitimate (Schaberg) or naturally born (Aus, Crossan, and Borg) but still think "fulfillment" is an appropriate term. For Schaberg, the idea of God overcoming Mary's disgrace is a more fitting "fulfillment" of the scriptural parallels than an unprecedented virginal conception. For Aus, it is Matthew's way of demonstrating that Jesus is Israel's final redeemer, based on stories and traditions concerning the birth of Moses. Neither thinks that Matthew and Luke were responsible for turning this into a miraculous virginal conception; that was the work of the later church and needs to be challenged. Crossan and Borg think that Matthew and Luke are not so easily exonerated but nevertheless agree that "fulfillment" is an appropriate word since the story "decisively reveals and incarnates the passion of God as disclosed in the Law and the Prophets—the promise and hope for a very different kind of world from the world of Pharaoh and Caesar, the world of domination and empire."[35]

The fourth view arose in critical scholarship around the mid-nineteenth century, when Bauer sought to "restore the marriage from which Jesus came as what it was—as a marriage that had already been consummated."[36] Interestingly, very few commentaries on Matthew's Gospel categorically deny the virginal conception but Luz calls it "quite improbable" and since this was not the original meaning of Isa 7:14, suggests that it is wrong to speak of "fulfillment."[37] In Bruce Chilton's imaginative "life of Jesus," he envisages Joseph traveling to Nazareth from nearby (Galilean) Bethlehem,[38] perhaps to

---

33. Hagner, *Matthew*, 20.

34. Keener, *Matthew*, 87.

35. Crossan and Borg, *First Christmas*, 224.

36. Cited in Luz, *Matthew 1–7*, 100.

37. Ibid., 100.

38. Chilton, *Rabbi Jesus*, 8–9. Chilton thinks this is the Bethlehem mentioned in Josh 19:15 and lies just seven miles from Nazareth. This became confused with the Judean Bethlehem when Mic 5:2 was used as a proof-text.

do repairs on Mary's house. They were soon betrothed but did not wait until they lived together to have sex. This was not in itself a scandal, but in order to "shield her from Nazareth's wagging tongues," Joseph took her to his house in Bethlehem to have the baby. Thus Jesus grew up under the suspicion of being a *mamzer*, an outcast of unknown paternity, and Chilton sees this as significant for understanding the figure we find in the Gospels:

> A critical, independent child with an ironic turn of mind, Jesus must have spent much of his time alone, wandering through the hills of Galilee, talking to the shepherds and vagrant rabbis who were regarded as shady characters in small communities like Nazareth. All the while, without training or conscious articulation, he was developing a sense of Israelite society that was radically inclusive and a vision of God that was not limited to the strictures of local institutions.[39]

To my mind, solution one is the least likely, as I cannot see how Isa 7:14 can be understood as predicting a virginal conception in the distant future, without disregarding the basic rules of vocabulary and grammar. Equally, for those who insist that "fulfillment" must involve "prediction," as most modern people probably would, then solution four is the only viable option, especially as a virginal conception goes against modern scientific knowledge. However, these writings come from the first century, when words like "fulfillment" were taken in a much broader sense, and so it would be unfair (and anachronistic) to insist that Matthew and Luke conform to modern modes of thought. On this view, some of the scholars mentioned in solution two might well be correct, though I am more hesitant than Brown to completely dismiss solution three. It goes against nearly 2,000 years of church tradition and some will find it blasphemous, but as Schaberg has shown, it does explain a number of points that otherwise seem odd (women in the genealogy, overcoming humiliation, shown mercy).

On the other hand, I think Brown is correct that it is very unlikely that this is what Matthew and Luke were trying to convey. Schaberg is correct that we must be careful not to simply read these stories in the light of church tradition but even setting that aside, many still find it difficult to see what she does. The question then is whether Matthew and Luke knew that Jesus was illegitimate and tried to cover it up with a theory of virginal conception, or that they both received this idea from traditions handed down to them? If they were writing independently, as most scholars believe,

39. Chilton, *Rabbi Jesus*, 17.

then the latter is more likely, as it would be quite a coincidence for both of them to fasten on such an unprecedented explanation. This means that the tradition must have developed fairly soon after Mark's Gospel, so as to be both available and authoritative for Matthew and Luke. Brown thinks this period is too short for such a momentous development to be credible and thinks that it tips the balance in favor of the historicity of the virginal conception. On the other hand, it is difficult to explain the complete silence on the subject until Matthew and Luke wrote their gospels some 70–80 years after Jesus' birth. Despite the desire to find something that "tips the balance," perhaps it is better not to go beyond the evidence and repeat Brown's conclusion: the historical evidence for a virginal conception is very thin but none of the alternative theories are especially convincing.[40]

40. Brown, *Birth of the Messiah,* 527. Lincoln's conclusion is that the illegitimacy reading "needs to be taken seriously as a minority report that raises significant questions about the traditional reading, questions that should cause the latter's adherents to re-think its justification, but that, on balance, it is not compelling enough to make them abandon it. Matthew, though obliquely, probably remains a witness to a virginal conception" ("Contested Paternity," 229).

6

Conclusion

WE SAW IN THE introduction that a trajectory can be constructed from early writings like Paul and Mark, which show no interest in Jesus' birth, to later writings like the Infancy Gospels of James and Thomas, which describe all manner of supernatural events. The question we posed was where do the infancy narratives of Matthew and Luke belong on this trajectory? Scholars such as Spong, Aus, Crossan, and Borg would place them towards the apocryphal literature, with the annunciations, births, star, magi, gifts, songs, and travel plans all created to illustrate the theological (and political) significance of Jesus. They deny that any form of deception was involved: it was simply the medium that came most naturally to them. Thus for Aus, Matthew's account is a "typically Jewish Christian haggadic embellishment of the birth of Israel's final redeemer," based on stories of the birth of Israel's first redeemer.[1] Crossan and Borg are more general, stating that a variety of scriptural models were utilized in order to show that Jesus "incarnates the passion of God as disclosed in the Law and the Prophets—the promise and hope for a very different kind of world from the world of Pharaoh and Caesar, the world of domination and empire."[2]

As they see it, the problem is that this form of communication was soon forgotten and the narratives were taken as literal descriptions of historical events. It was then necessary to show that the scriptural quotations are actual predictions, which were fulfilled in the specific events

1. Aus, *Matthew 1–2*, 84.
2. Crossan and Borg, *The First Christmas*, 224.

102

surrounding Jesus' birth. Not surprisingly, this has led to two quite opposite positions. Conservative scholars like Sailhamer and Kaiser have attempted to show that if the wider context of the quotations is taken into account, then the texts *can* be understood as messianic predictions. Most scholars, however, regard this as special pleading and think that a predictive meaning can only be understood by violating the normal rules of vocabulary and grammar. For Luz, this means that we should no longer speak of "fulfillment," though he recognizes that the stories contain significant insights into the person of Jesus.

Another group of scholars think that the infancy narratives of Matthew and Luke should be placed towards the beginning of the trajectory, arguing that they are in touch with history even though their primary purpose is theological. Interestingly, the conclusion that the quotations were not predictions in their original context becomes an argument for the historicity of some of the traditions. Evans, for example, argues that it is very unlikely that non-predictive texts like Hos 11:1 ("out of Egypt") and Jer 31:15 ("weeping in Ramah") would have generated the "flight to Egypt" and "slaughter of the innocents" stories. It is much more likely that Matthew drew on historical traditions and then found these texts in order to give theological meaning to the events. He is even prepared to extend this argument to Mic 5:2 ("ruler from Bethlehem") and Isa 7:14 ("virgin will conceive"), since there is no evidence that anyone in the first century took these as predictions. In other words, it would hardly have served an apologetic purpose to invent stories that fulfilled texts that no one thought needed fulfilling. Thus Evans can speak of typological fulfillment because he thinks that most of the events really happened, even though the quotations are not predictions in their original contexts. As we noted earlier, France suggests that Matthew

> expresses in the most economical form a wide-ranging theology of the new exodus and of Jesus as the true Israel which will play a significant role throughout Matthew's gospel. As usual, Matthew's christological interpretation consists not of exegesis of what the text quoted meant in its original context, but of a far-reaching theological argument which takes the OT text and locates it within an over-arching scheme of fulfillment which finds in Jesus the end point of numerous prophetic trajectories. When Jesus "came out of Egypt," that was to be the signal for a new exodus in which Jesus

would fill the role not only of the God-sent deliverer but also of God's "son" Israel himself.[3]

But what if Jesus never went to Egypt? Can we speak of typological fulfillment if there is no historical event to correspond with the non-predictive (but suggestive) biblical text? On one level, the answer is clearly no, because there is nothing to offer as a parallel to the original exodus event. However, most scholars would agree that the claim to typological fulfillment is not really about geography but whether Jesus initiated a movement that *figuratively* brings people out of Egypt and *figuratively* brings them into a promised land. If that belief is held, then it is possible to see a trajectory from the original exodus, Hosea's figurative use of the exodus tradition to describe the restoration of Israel, and Matthew's understanding of what Jesus accomplished. Indeed, it is only on such a belief that one can understand John the Baptist as the forerunner (Mal 3:1) who prepares the way of the Lord (Isa 40:3) or the genealogies as affirming that Jesus is the promised "Son of David," despite the lack of agreement in the names of his ancestors.

It might come as a disappointment that we cannot give an objective answer to the question, "Was the Birth of Jesus according to Scripture?" Is it not the task of scholarship to settle such questions and to settle them once and for all? However, a moment's reflection will show that this could never be the case with questions such as these. If one does not believe that in some way or another Jesus represents the "promise and hope for a very different kind of world," as Crossan and Borg put it, then concepts like typological fulfillment will seem like special pleading. But for those who do think of Jesus in such terms, then there is the possibility of accepting the word "fulfillment" in one of the ways described in this book. Some will wish to follow scholars like Evans and France and accept the historicity of much of what we read in Matthew and Luke; others will prefer a more symbolic approach. All agree, however, that the scriptural background presented in Matthew and Luke provides invaluable insights into the person of Jesus and is therefore worthy of study. It is my hope that reading this book has helped you to come to the same conclusion, whatever understanding of "fulfillment" you decide is the most likely or the most plausible.

3. France, *Matthew*, 81.

Bibliography

Allison, D. C. *The New Moses: A Matthean Typology.* Minneapolis: Augsburg Fortress, 1993.

Aus, R. D. *Matthew 1–2 and the Virginal Conception: In Light of Palestinian and Hellenistic Judaic Traditions on the Birth of Israel's First Redeemer, Moses.* Lanham, MD: University Press of America, 2004.

Barrett, C. K. *The Gospel according to St John: An Introduction with Commentary and Notes on the Greek Text.* London: SPCK, 1955.

Beale, G. K. *The Book of Revelation.* NIGTC. Grand Rapids: Eerdmans, 1999.

———. *Handbook on the New Testament Use of the Old Testament: Exegesis and Interpretation.* Grand Rapids: Baker Academic, 2012.

———. *A New Testament Biblical Theology: The Unfolding of the Old Testament in the New.* Grand Rapids: Baker Academic, 2011.

Becking, B. *Between Fear and Freedom. Essays on the Interpretation of Jeremiah 30–31.* Leiden: Brill, 2004.

Bird, M. F. *Are you the One to Come?: The Historical Jesus and the Messianic Question.* Grand Rapids: Baker Academic, 2009.

Blomberg, C. L. "Matthew." In *Commentary on the New Testament Use of the Old Testament,* edited by G. K. Beale and D. A. Carson, 1–109. Grand Rapids: Baker, 2007.

Bock, D. L. *Proclamation from Prophecy and Pattern: Lucan Old Testament Christology.* JSNTSup 12; Sheffield, UK: Sheffield Academic, 1987.

Borg, M. J., and J. D. Crossan. *The First Christmas: What the Gospels Really Teach about Jesus' Birth.* Kindle edition. New York: HarperOne, 2009.

Brooke, G. J., editor. *The Birth of Jesus: Biblical and Theological Reflections.* Edinburgh: T. & T. Clark, 2000.

Brown, R. *The Birth of the Messiah: A Commentary of the Infancy Narratives in the Gospels of Matthew and Luke.* 2nd ed. Garden City, NY: Doubleday, 1993.

Bruner, F. D. *Matthew: The Christbook, Matthew 1–12.* Rev. ed. Grand Rapids: Eerdmans, 2004.

Byrne, M. *The Way It Was: The Narrative of the Birth of Jesus.* Dublin: Columba, 2004.

Casey, P. M. *An Aramaic Approach to Q.* SNTSMS, 122. Cambridge: Cambridge University Press, 2002.

Charlesworth, J. H., editor. *The Old Testament Pseudepigrapha.* Vol 1: Apocalyptic Literature and Testaments. London: Darton, Longman and Todd, 1983.

Chilton, B. *Rabbi Jesus: An Intimate Biography.* Garden City, NY: Doubleday, 2000.

Clarke, H. *The Gospel of Matthew and its Readers.* Bloomington, IN: Indiana University Press, 2003.

Corley, J. *New Perspectives on the Nativity.* T. & T. Clark, 2009.

Davidson, H. *T. S. Eliot and Hermeneutics: Absence and Interpretation in "The Waste Land."* Baton Rouge: Louisiana State University Press, 1985.

Davies, W. D., and D. C. Allison. *A Critical and Exegetical Commentary on the Gospel according to Saint Matthew 1: Commentary on Matthew I–VII.* ICC. Edinburgh: T. & T. Clark, 1988.

———. *A Critical and Exegetical Commentary on the Gospel according to Saint Matthew 2: Commentary on Matthew VIII–XVIII.* ICC. Edinburgh: T. & T. Clark, 1991.

———. *A Critical and Exegetical Commentary on the Gospel according to Saint Matthew 3: Commentary on Matthew. XVIX–XXVIII.* ICC. Edinburgh: T. & T. Clark, 1997.

Dodd, C. H. *The Interpretation of the Fourth Gospel.* Cambridge: Cambridge University Press, 1953.

Ehrman, B. D. *The New Testament: A Historical Introduction to the Early Christian Writings.* 5th ed. New York: Oxford University Press, 2011.

Elliott, J. K. *The Apocryphal New Testament.* Oxford: Oxford University Press, 1993.

Erickson, R. J. "Divine Injustice?: Matthew's Narrative Strategy and the Slaughter of the Innocents (Matthew 2.13–23)." *Journal for the Study of the New Testament* 64 (1996) 5–27.

Evans, C. A. "The Messiah in the Old and New Testaments: A Response." In *The Messiah in the Old and New Testaments,* edited by S. E. Porter, 230–48. Grand Rapids: Eerdmans, 2007.

Fitzmyer, J. A. *The Gospel according to Luke X–XXIV.* Anchor Bible 28; Garden City, NY: Doubleday, 1986.

France, R. T. *The Gospel of Mark.* Grand Rapids: Eerdmans, 2002.

———. *The Gospel of Matthew.* NICNT. Grand Rapids: Eerdmans, 2007.

———. "The 'Massacre of the Innocents'—Fact or Fiction?" In *Studia Biblica 1978. II. Papers on the Gospels,* edited by E. A. Livingstone, 83–94. Sheffield, UK: JSOT, 1980.

Freed, E. D. *The Stories of Jesus' Birth.* London: Continuum, 2004.

Green, J. B. *The Gospel of Luke.* Grand Rapids: Eerdmans, 1997.

———. *The Theology of the Gospel of Luke.* Cambridge: Cambridge University Press, 1995.

Gundry, R. H. *Matthew: A Commentary on His Handbook for a Mixed Church under Persecution.* Grand Rapids: Eerdmans, 1994.

———. *The Use of the Old Testament in St. Matthew's Gospel, with Special Reference to the Messianic Hope.* NovTSup 18. Leiden: Brill, 1975.

Hagner, D. *Matthew.* Dallas: Word, 1993.

Hays, R. B. "The Gospel of Matthew: Reconfigured Torah." *Harvard Theological Studies* 61 (2005) 165–90.

Horbury, W. *Jewish Messianism and the Cult of Christ.* London: SCM, 1998.

Horsley, R. *The Liberation of Christmas: The Infancy Narratives in Social Context.* New York: Crossroad, 1989.

Jassen, A. P. *Mediating the Divine: Prophecy and Revelation in the Dead Sea Scrolls and Second Temple Judaism.* Leiden: Brill, 2007.

Johnson, L. T. *The Gospel of Luke: A Commentary on the Greek Text.* Collegeville, MN: Liturgical, 1991.

Kaiser, W. C. *The Uses of the Old Testament in the New.* Chicago: Moody, 1985.

Keener, C. S. *A Commentary on the Gospel of Matthew*. Grand Rapids: Eerdmans, 1999.

Kelly, J. F. *The Birth of Jesus according to the Gospels*. Collegeville, MN: Order of Saint Benedict, 2008.

Knight, J. *Luke's Gospel*. London: Routledge, 1998.

Kupp, D. *Matthew's Emmanuel: Divine Presence and God's People in the First Gospel*. SNTSMS 90; Cambridge: Cambridge University Press, 1996.

Lincoln, A. T. "Contested Paternity and Contested Readings: Jesus' Conception in Matthew 1.18-25." *Journal for the Study of the New Testament* 34 (2012) 211–31.

Luz, U. *Matthew 1-7: A Commentary*. Translated by W. C. Linss. Minneapolis: Augsburg, 1989.

Marcus, J. *The Way of the Lord: Christological Exegesis of the Old Testament in the Gospel of Mark*. Edinburgh: T. & T. Clark, 1980.

Marshall, I. H. *The Gospel of Luke: A Commentary on the Greek Text*. NIGTC. Exeter, UK: Paternoster, 1978.

McCartney, D., and P. Enns. "Matthew and Hosea: A Response to John Sailhamer." *Westminster Theological Journal* 63 (2001) 97–105.

Menken, M. J. J. *Matthew's Bible: The Old Testament Text of the Evangelist*. BETL 173. Leuven: Peeters, 2004.

Miller, R. J. *Born Divine: The Birth of Jesus and other Sons of God*. Santa Rosa: Polebridge, 2002.

Moyise, S. *Evoking Scripture: Seeing the Old Testament in the New*. London: T. & T. Clark, 2008.

—————. *The Later New Testament Writers and Scripture*. London: SPCK, 2012.

—————. *The Old Testament in the New*. London: T. & T. Clark, 2001.

Nolland, J. *The Gospel of Matthew: A Commentary on the Greek Text*. NIGTC. Grand Rapids: Eerdmans, 2005.

—————. *Luke 1:1—9:20*. Word Biblical Commentary. Dallas: Word, 1989.

O'Toole, R. F. *Luke's Presentation of Jesus: A Christology*. Rome: EPIB, 2004.

Pesch, R. "'He will be called a Nazorean': Messianic Exegesis in Matthew 1-2." In *The Gospels and the Scriptures of Israel*, edited by C. Evans and W. R. Stenger, 129–78. Sheffield, UK: JSOT, 1994.

Pietersma, A., and B. G.Wright, editors. *New English Translation of the Septuagint*. New York: Oxford University Press, 2007.

Porter, S. E., editor. *The Messiah in the Old and New Testaments*. Grand Rapids: Eerdmans, 2007.

Puskas, C. B., and D. Crump. *An Introduction to the Gospels and Acts*. Grand Rapids: Eerdmans, 2008.

Sailhamer, J. "Hosea 11:1 and Matthew 2:15." *Westminster Theological Journal* 63 (2001) 87–96.

Sanders, J. A. "Nazoraios in Matthew 2.23." In *The Gospels and the Scriptures of Israel*, edited by C. Evans and W. R. Stenger, 116–128. Sheffield, UK: JSOT, 1994.

Schaberg, J. *The Illegitimacy of Jesus: A Feminist Theological Interpretation of the Infancy Narratives*. Sheffield, UK: Sheffield Academic Press, 1995.

Soares Prabhu, G. M. *The Formula Quotations in the Infancy Narrative of Matthew: An Enquiry into the Tradition History of Mt 1-2*. Analecta biblica 63; Rome: Biblical Institute Press, 1976.

Sperber, D., and D. Wilson. *Relevance: Communication and Cognition*. 2nd ed. Oxford: Blackwell, 1995.

Bibliography

Spong, J. S. *Born of a Woman: A Bishop Rethinks the Birth of Jesus.* New York: HarperCollins, 1992.

Starcky, J. "Les Quatres Étapes du Messianisme à Qumrân." *Revue biblique* 70 (1963) 487–505.

Stendahl, K. "Quis et Unde? An Analysis of Mt 1–2." In *Judentum, Urchristentum, Kirche: Festschrift für Joachim Jeremias,* edited by W. Eltester, 94–105. Berlin: Töpelmann, 1960.

————. *The School of St. Matthew and Its Use of the Old Testament.* Philadelphia: Fortress, 1968.

Sternberg, M. "Proteus in Quotation-Land: Mimesis and the Forms of Reported Discourse." *Poetics Today* 3 (1982) 107–56.

Stromberg, J. *An Introduction to the Study of Isaiah.* London: T. & T. Clark, 2011.

Talbert, C. H. *Reading Luke.* New York: Crossroad, 1982.

Turner, D. L. *Matthew.* BECNT. Grand Rapids: Baker Academic, 2008.

Vermes, G. *The Complete Dead Sea Scrolls.* Rev. ed. London: Penguin, 2004.

Watts, R. "Mark." In *Commentary on the New Testament Use of the Old Testament,* edited by G. K. Beale and D. A. Carson, 111–249. Grand Rapids: Baker Academic, 2007.

Weren, W. "Quotations from Isaiah and Matthew's Christology (Mt 1,23 and 4,15–16)." In *Studies in the Book of Isaiah: Festschrift Willem A. M. Beuken,* edited by J. van Ruiten and M. Vervenne, 447–65. BETL 132; Leuven: Peeters, 1997.

Biblical References

Was the Birth of Jesus According to Scripture?

Luke

Revelation

Modern Authors

117